Amphibians and Reptiles
of New England

The University of Massachusetts Press

Amherst

Amphibians and Reptiles of New England

Habitats and Natural History

Richard M. DeGraaf
Deborah D. Rudis
Drawings by Abigail Rorer

Copyright © 1983 by

The University of Massachusetts Press

All rights reserved

Printed in the United States of America

Designed by Mary Mendell

Library of Congress Cataloging in Publication Data

DeGraaf, Richard M.

Amphibians and reptiles of New England.

Bibliography: p.

Includes index.

1. Reptiles—New England. 2. Amphibians—New

England. I. Rudis, Deborah D. II. Title.

QL653.N35D43 1983 597.6'0974 83–5125

ISBN 0–87023–400–5 (pbk.)

Contents

Acknowledgments

We gratefully acknowledge those who helped in this work. Michael W. Klemens of the American Museum of Natural History in New York deserves special credit as technical consultant. He was also a reviewer of the original manuscript and his expertise was invaluable for the completion of this book. The following also willingly reviewed the original manuscript and made many useful suggestions: Thomas J. Andrews, University of Massachusetts, Amherst, Terry E. Graham, Worcester State College, Worcester, Massachusetts, James D. Lazell, The Conservation Agency, Conanicut Island, Rhode Island, Margaret M. Stewart, State University of New York at Albany, and Thomas F. Tyning, Massachusetts Audubon Society, Pittsfield, Massachusetts.

Thanks are also due to the following people for providing access to collections at their institutions: Doug Smith (University of Massachusetts, Amherst), Edward Malante and Thomas Uzzell (Academy of Natural Science, Philadelphia), Jose Rosado (Museum of Comparative Zoology, Harvard), and Bill Glans and Mickey Marcus (University of Maine, Orono).

Special mention is due to staff members of the Natural Heritage Program of the Nature Conservancy in New England: Judy Harding (Massachusetts), Christopher Raithel (Rhode Island), Marc DesMeules (Vermont and New Hampshire), Tom French and Larry Master (New England); their assistance on numerous occasions is gratefully acknowledged.

We give special thanks to Dorothy McDougal for patiently typing several drafts of the original manuscript. Robert E. Radtke and David T. Funk, USDA Forest Service, provided administrative support.

Jim Lockyer, Northeastern Forest Experiment Station, rendered the forest-type map. William Hauser, U.S. Forest Service, supplied the photographs of forest types.

Among the many others who helped with this book by providing information or offering their encouragement, we would like to thank especially Dolores E. DeGraaf, Edward and Patricia Rudis, and Nicholas W. Sampson.

Preface

This book is a guide to the natural history and habitats of the inland amphibians and reptiles of New England. It is a guide for wildlife biologists and naturalists, both professionals and students, whose responsibilities or interests require access to a concise summary of herpetofaunal life-history information

The habitat associations of amphibians and reptiles are generally not as well known as are those of other terrestrial vertebrates. Indeed, we know little about the life history, status, and distribution of many species. Amphibians and reptiles are important components in the functioning of forest and other ecosystems, but they are often poorly represented in resource inventories and wildlife management plans because their habitat needs, and even their occurrences, are poorly described. Some species may be quite abundant, yet are rarely encountered due to their fossorial habits, nocturnal activities, or limited movements. Children readily find and keep salamanders, frogs, toads, turtles, and snakes, but often their curiosity wanes with adulthood, and this relative disinterest appears to hold true even among wildlife professionals.

Most public land-management agencies are bound by legislation and subsequent regulations to state the effects of their management practices on other resources, including wildlife. Our ability to describe or predict the effects of given forest management practices, for example, on reptiles and amphibians is fairly poor for most of these species; this is true either because their presence is often unknown or because as a group they have not been studied from a habitat perspective.

This book brings together information on the range, relative abundance in New England, habitat, key habitat requirements, breeding period, growth and development, home range and movements, food habits, and key references for each species. The introduction generally describes the physiography of New England.

While amphibian and reptile geographic distributions are more frequently related to soil type, climate, or presence of water, and tend to be less directly related to forest or vegetation type, such associations have seldom been critically studied or even summarized before. Inasmuch as the size, distribution, and variety of wildlife populations are functions of the amount, diversity, and quality of available habitats (among other factors), sound wildlife management is largely dependent upon the systematic accumulation and analysis of habitat data. Amphibians and reptiles, especially in New England, have not been adequately related to habitat classification schemes to the extent that they can be considered in land-management planning.

This is not a field guide for species identification. Two such guides are Roger Conant, *A Field Guide to Reptiles and Amphibians of Eastern and Central North America* (1957; reprint ed., Boston: Houghton Mifflin Co., 1975) and J. L. Behler and F. W. King, *The Audubon Society Field Guide to North American Reptiles and Amphibians* (New York: Alfred A. Knopf, 1979).

Scientific and common names follow those in *Standard Common and Current Scientific Names for North American Amphibians and Reptiles* (Collins et al. 1982). Measurements are provided in the units used in the original work. When the earlier text used U.S. units, metric equivalents have been supplied.

Introduction

This book presents information on the natural history of amphibians and reptiles that occur in New England, although it often has wider geographic applications. We assembled this material from the literature, reviews, consultations with experts, and continuing field research. The life-history accounts are based on available studies conducted in New England. Where information from states outside the region is included, we attempted to note the locality of the research in the text. Often life-history information is incomplete or unavailable; further research is needed to fill in the gaps in our knowledge. Key life-history references are listed at the end of each species account. They are not necessarily the most recent references, but are included because they are the most complete general references available.

The relative abundance indicated in each species account is an approximation. More specific information is provided for some species in the special status tables. Included in the habitat section are details from knowledgeable local herpetologists. Habitat use during breeding and hibernation periods is summarized in this section, and, if specific habitat components are required by a species, they are listed under "Special Habitat Requirements." The "Comments" section provides additional information to better acquaint the user with each species.

The fifty-six amphibians and reptiles in this guide were selected because New England is included in all or part of their range. Of these, the mudpuppy *(Necturus maculosus)* and red-eared slider *(Pseudemys scripta elegans)* are introduced species that have established populations in parts of the region.

This guide is limited to inland (nonmarine) amphibians and reptiles of New England. However, the natural-history profiles of these species include information from other northeastern states. Thus the text is useful for areas outside New England where those species and habitats are found.

There have been other inland species reported from New England. We have included the mountain dusky salamander *(Desmognathus ochrophaeus)*. Reported from a single Vermont specimen (Lazell 1976b), its identification has yet to be generally accepted.

Specimens of the Eastern mud turtle *(Kinosternon s. subrubrum)* found in Connecticut are believed to have been released (Craig 1979); no breeding populations are known at this time, thus we have omitted the species from consideration.

Two records of the rough green snake *(Opheodrys aestivus)* exist for Connecticut. Lamson (1935) reported a specimen from Waterbury and there is a specimen from West Haven (1943) from the W. F. Prince Collection at the University of Massachusetts. We do not believe, however, that its inclusion here is warranted.

Within the geographic area of New England there are species that are rare or uncommon in one area, but that are fairly common in another. Some species are at or near the limits of their geographic range. "Limiting factors" may include such climatic considerations as the amount of rainfall, maximum-minimum temperature ranges, or depth of frost, and such physical factors as soil type, plant community, and topography.

Disjunct populations, isolated from the contiguous range of a species, may occur as remnant or relict populations of a formerly more widespread species, such as Blanding's turtle (*Emydoidea blandingii*) (Bleakney 1958). Some isolated populations, such as those of the timber rattlesnake (*Crotalus horridus*) are due to recent habitat loss and man's attempts at species eradication. Other isolated populations are the result of changes in the environment that left only patches of favorable habitat. It is essential to protect these habitats to preserve outlying populations.

A map of each species's approximate distribution in New England is included with its natural-history profile. The shading of each species's map shows the extent of its presumed continuous range. Maps were derived from the literature and museum specimens.

County records for each species, most documented by museum specimens, have been indicated on its map as solid circles. These circles represent only county records; they do not represent exact locations. Open circles indicate that, although historic records exist, no specimens have been recently reported.

A historical perspective

New England does not have a body of herpetological literature like that available for other parts of the country. Compared to much of the rest of the contiguous United States, the herpetofauna of New England is not very diverse. When early English travelers recorded their impressions of the amphibians and reptiles of the area, factual information was often embellished with fantasy and exaggeration. Most colonial records particularly note rattlesnake encounters. In 1622 the king of the Narragansett Indians sent a warning in the form of a rattler's skin filled with arrows to Governor Bradford of Plymouth Plantation. Bradford returned the skin filled with musket shot (Babcock 1921). In *New England's Prospect* (1634) William Wood provided some accurate observations of the rattlesnake, the "most sleepy and unnimble creature that lives; never offering to leap or bite any man, if he not be trodden on first. . . ." In *New England Rarities* (1672), John Josselyn, a visitor from England, described some of the more common species encountered during his 1663 voyage to New England. Closely following Wood, he noted, "the 'pond-frogs'" which "chirp in Spring like Sparrows and croke like Toads in Autumn," and recounted that Indians "up in the country" find "Pond-frogs as big as a child of a year old" (people were smaller in the 1600s!). Rattlesnakes are described as "carrying stings in their tails," in Josselyn's *An Account of Two Voyages to New England* (1675). The "eft or swift . . . painted with glorious colours" is probably a five-lined skink.

Later accounts of the herpetofauna of New England sent to English scientific societies were not necessarily more accurate. Captain Walduck's letter of 1714 to the Royal Society of London discussed rattlesnakes as possessing a "wonderfull Fascination," enabling them to "charm them, both Squirrels & Birds into their mouths from ye top of a Tree 50 foot high . . ." (Masterson 1938).

It was not until the 1830s that significant records of species and comments on life history began to appear. Much of the early information on amphibians and reptiles in New England was primarily published as state or local faunal lists. Frequently, reports were catalogues with descriptions of specimens submitted to state natural history societies such as the Boston and Portland Societies of Natural History. The notes of Linsley (1843) from Connecticut, J. A. Allen (1870) for Massachusetts, Fogg (1862) and Verrill (1863) for Maine, and G. M. Allen (1899) for New Hampshire are examples of such catalogues. Zadock Thompson's *Natural History of Vermont* (1853) was the first publication to accurately describe the herpetofauna of that state. Publications of the Roger Williams Park Museum of Rhode Island and the Connecticut Geological and Natural History Survey include reports of Drowne (1905), Lamson (1935), and Babbitt (1937). Several of these catalogues contain questionable records that do not refer to a specific locality or to specimens. They include reports of the tiger salamander and five-lined skink (blue-tailed lizard) in Maine (Fogg 1862), and the worm and black rat (pilot black) snakes in New Hampshire (Henshaw 1904).

Other unusual location records, verified by these early authors (who also examined the specimens) deserve mention. They include a worm snake from Maine examined by J. A.

Allen (1868), a marbled salamander from Milford, New Hampshire (Hoopes 1938), and MacCoy's mention (1931) of tiger salamander specimens from Harwichport and Hanover, Massachusetts.

The first attempt at a complete list of amphibians and reptiles was Smith's catalogue in Hitchcock's *Report on the Geology, Mineralogy, Botany, and Zoology of Massachusetts* (1835). Smith listed seven turtles, ten snakes, nine frogs and toads, and seven "Salamanders or Slows." Storer's report (1840) to the Massachusetts legislature followed, and contained species descriptions and comments on the habits and habitats of species in the state. J. A. Allen's notes (1868) on the herpetofauna of Springfield, Massachusetts, alluded to decreasing numbers from habitat loss, "draining of ponds and marshes . . . destruction of the forests . . . and the burning of newly cleared lands." Allen discusses the needless destruction of snakes, which reduced species, common in Springfield only ten to fifteen years earlier, to scarcity or "great rarities." It is interesting to note his comments regarding the excessive number of species of salamanders, where variations rather than true species are described.

In the early 1900s, individual species accounts were commonly published in New England's scientific journals. Many of these include historic locations, notes on habits, habitats, and behavioral observations. The black rat snake (MacCoy 1930), American and Fowler's toads (Hoopes 1930), copperhead (Babcock 1926), wood frog (Hinckley 1882), and spring peeper (Hinckley 1883), among others, were described in this manner.

Oliver and Bailey's "Amphibians and Reptiles of New Hampshire" in *Biological Survey of the Connecticut Watershed* (1939) was the most complete discussion of the herpetofauna for any of the New England states up to that time: life history, habitat notes, and location records from both the literature and extensive field work were included. Unfortunately, no parallel work exists for New England as a whole. Publications dealing with faunal groups of the area exist, however, such as Babcock's *Snakes of New England* (1929) and *Turtles of New England* (1919). Dunn's *Salamanders of the Family Plethodontidae* (1926) encompassed species of New England and the southern Appalachians. An excellent account of venomous snakes of Connecticut is Petersen's publication (1970). More local in scope is Lazell's *This Broken Archipelago* (1976) concerning the herpetofauna of Cape Cod. Conant's *Reptiles and Amphibians of the Northeastern States* (1957) is a popular pamphlet rather than a full reference.

Spruce-Fir

Physiography and vegetation

New England's generally leveled, rolling topography is the northeastern extension of the Appalachian Highlands, largely consisting of upland plateaus 305–610 m (1,000–2,000 ft) in elevation. This so-called peneplain matrix is frequently interrupted by mountain peaks and valley lowlands.

When the last of four Pleistocene glaciers to cover New England, the Wisconsin, retreated, it left a scoured and debris-covered landscape. The present-day herpetofaunal distribution of the region resulted from postglacial immigrations from unglaciated areas or refugia. The Mississippi Valley, Atlantic Coastal Plain, and Appalachian Mountains were the three major dispersal routes by which amphibians and reptiles reached New England. Bleakney (1958) states that many of the boreal species did not follow a specific dispersal route from their probable refugia in the southern Appalachians, but dispersed east, west, and north.

The mountains of New England are eroded remnants of earlier cycles of uplift and erosion. Many occur as monadnocks—peaks of resistant rock projecting above surrounding peneplains. The major mountain ranges are the Taconic Mountains and Berkshire Hills of western Massachusetts and northwestern Connecticut, the Green Mountains of Vermont and western Massachusetts, and the White Mountains of New Hampshire. The Presidential Range of the White Mountains, the highest range in the Northeast, includes Mt. Washington at 1,917 m (6,290 ft) and four other peaks above 1,615 m (5,300 ft).

Northern Hardwoods-Spruce

Geologically, New England is very old—some of the oldest metamorphic rock formations in the world are found throughout the region. The mountains and upland plateaus are primarily composed of granite, gneisses, and schists. The bedrock is granitic and so contains a high proportion of quartz. Thus, generally, soils are moderately coarse textured, acidic, and of relatively low fertility. In the valleys, fine textured soils that have resulted from calcareous parent material are much more fertile.

Glaciation has produced profound changes, however, and the resultant manner in which the transported debris or drift was deposited largely determines soil fertility. Because soils did not develop in place, New England is not simply a region of infertile uplands grading into fertile valleys. Often the best soils for forest development consist of unsorted glacial drift (till) deposited by glacial withdrawal. Such soils are frequently found on midslopes of hills and mountains. Conversely, water-transported drift, frequently stratified and deposited in broad outwash plains and glacial lake shores, often produced poor soils at lower elevations.

Till soils throughout New England frequently contain a relatively impervious compact layer, or fragipan, several inches to a foot or more below the surface. Vernal pools, seeps, and wet ground, even on upper slopes, are common in spring due to the presence of this layer.

Disrupted drainage patterns, scoured-out glacial basins, and glacially dammed waterways have created many ponds and lakes. The melting of ice blocks, buried in glacial debris, created depressions that formed kettle-hole lakes, especially on Cape Cod. Wetlands and bogs have formed in smaller, shallower depressions (Barrett 1962:37–38). Vernal pools and kettle-hole ponds, along with other wetlands, are used by mole salamanders, the Ambystomids, for breeding sites. These sites afford an aquatic environment that is often temporary, reducing the number of predators, e.g., fish, that would be found in larger or permanent water bodies. Spadefoot toads frequently breed in kettle-hole ponds, in areas of sandy soil.

Soils are of two related types. True podzols, which are quite acidic, and contain a highly leached, whitish-gray layer, are found in northern New England and at higher elevations in southern New England. They are coarse, and are associated with abundant precipitation, cool climate, and coniferous forests. The heavier brown or gray-brown weak pozdols, generally characteristic of southern New England, are associated with warmer climate and hardwood forests.

Climate and weather

New England is typically cool and humid—the climate is continental rather than maritime except for areas near the Atlantic Coast. Prevailing westerly winds and Canadian air masses dominate the region's weather far more than the Atlantic Ocean does. Precipitation averages 100 cm annually. The number of frost-free days ranges from 150 to 155 in southern Connecticut and 100 to 120 in northern Maine. Average maximum temperatures are 22 c for southern Connecticut and 19 c for northern Maine. Average minimum temperatures vary greatly, ranging from -2 c in Connecticut to -15 c in Maine.

Northern Hardwoods

Forest cover

Forests cover over 80% of the total land area of New England; there are over 32,491,000 acres of forest land (U.S. Dept. of Agric. 1977). The forests that cover New England can be grouped into six major community types or zones. Representative tree species of each type are the basis for community names. Both gradual transitions and abrupt boundaries occur between types, depending upon soil conditions, slope, and aspect or exposure. Within distinct forest zones are islands and belts characteristic of other types, reflecting conditions more favorable to these communities. Amphibian and reptile communities vary with these forest communities; some species are specific to particular types, others are ubiquitous.

Forest community zones described here are based on Kuchler's *Potential Natural Vegetation* (1964). Kuchler's work was used and expanded in *Land Resource Regions and Major Land Resource Areas of the United States,* by the USDA, Soil Conservation Service (1981).

The spruce-fir type comprises almost 30% of all forest land in New England (USDA, Forest Service 1977). In the spruce-fir zone, balsam fir and red spruce are the major forest species. Black spruce is found in bogs and swamps, white spruce is associated with abandoned fields. Red maple, paper birch, quaking and big tooth aspen, and mountain-ash are common hardwood components. Other conifers of this zone are tamarack and hemlock. Krummholz is characteristic at high altitudes.

The northern hardwoods-spruce forest zone contains mainly beech, white and yellow birch, sugar maple, and hemlock on better drained

Transition Zone

Appalachian Oak

soils. (Hemlock is only found at lower elevations in northern New England.) Wetter soils, mountain tops, and northern aspects are characterized by spruce and fir stands. Hardwood stands with scattered white pine and hemlock are generally on southern aspects. White pine stands are found on abandoned farmland in river valleys and outwash plains.

Hardwood forests comprise over 51% of all New England forest land, half of these 16,164,700 acres are northern hardwood (USDA, Forest Service 1977). The northern hardwood zone includes beech, sugar maple, and yellow birch. Hemlock, American elm, basswood, black cherry, and white ash are found less frequently. Early successional species of this zone are quaking and bigtooth aspen and birch. Red maple, American elm, hemlock, white cedar, and spruce are characteristic of wetter sites.

The eastern hardwood-pine forest is a transition zone. Northern birches, beech, and maples overlap the oaks and hickories associated with warmer and drier conditions. Hemlock is found in the northern and cooler sites within this zone. White pine is characteristic of lighter, sandy soils. Wetter soils support red maple, black ash, and American elm.

The Appalachian oak forest is a mixture of northern and central hardwoods. A variety of oaks and hickories, sugar maple, birches, and beech are major species. White pine and hemlock are the primary conifers. Red maple occurs on wetter sites. Pitch and red pine grow on sandy outwash soils. American chestnut was formerly the dominant tree species.

The northeastern oak-pine zone is composed of pitch pine, scrub oak, scarlet oak, and black oak. Frequent fires have created favorable conditions for pitch pine and scrub oak, and they occur almost exclusively in some areas. Early successional species in burned-over areas are lowbush blueberry and other ericaceous shrubs.

Since most New England amphibians require water for breeding, there may be no direct relationship between their occurrence and the forest community surrounding the breeding site. Indirect relationships occur when vegetative cover in riparian zones influences water temperature, pH, or the presence and type of bottom litter. Some species may be found in a wide range of forest community types if the required aquatic habitat component is present within those types. Some terrestrial microhabitats of forest communities may be equally important in determining species occurrence (Krysik 1980). In addition to wooded areas, streams and other aquatic locations (including bogs, marshes, wet meadows, and swamps), upland grassy communities, and nonvegetated areas (talus slopes, banks, beaches, and man-made structures) provide habitat for many species. Pollutants may impose a further limitation on occurrence of some species (Gochfeld 1975). The life histories and habitat accounts in this book include some examples. Further field research is necessary to determine more specifically the habitat relationships and distributions of amphibians and reptiles in New England. Some amphibians and reptiles are restricted to a narrow range of habitat conditions for breeding, feeding, or both; the bog turtle requires wetlands with high humidity and an open canopy, and the spadefoot is associated with the sandy soils of flood plains. Other

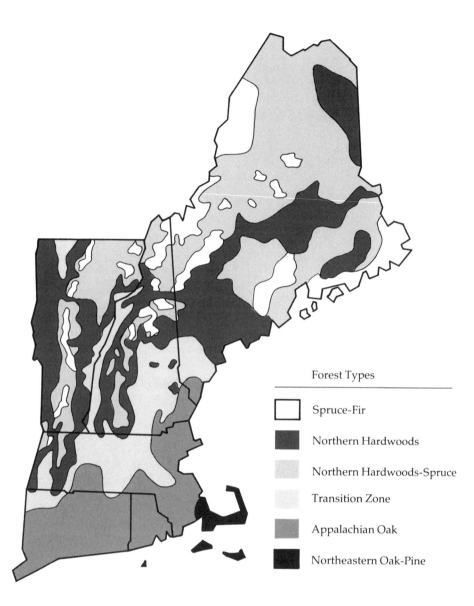

Forest Types

☐ Spruce-Fir

■ Northern Hardwoods

▨ Northern Hardwoods-Spruce

☐ Transition Zone

▨ Appalachian Oak

■ Northeastern Oak-Pine

species are more general in their requirements: wood frogs and American toads are found in a number of forest types, the redback salamander is common in a variety of habitats. Depending upon individual species's requirements, we can determine habitat associations for New England herpetofauna. Based on environmental conditions characteristic of forest community types and successional stages, the associated herpetofaunal assemblage can be generally described.

Amphibian and reptile status ratings

As public environmental awareness grows, more pressure is put on state and federal agencies to protect habitats and species. This has resulted in recent legislation in some of the New England states to fully protect some amphibians and reptiles, to regulate the taking of others for food, and to require collectors to obtain permits for their activities. Conservation organizations, notably the Nature Conservancy, have investigated the status of many species in the region; such information is available to those considering regulations or proposing legislation.

There are presently thirty-eight species and subspecies of amphibians and reptiles occurring within the six New England states that have been accorded special status. They are included on rare and endangered species lists developed by state and federal agencies or by special study groups. Species listings are provided on a state-by-state basis because the status designation in one state may differ from the status of a species in an adjacent state (tables 1 and 2). Standardized status definitions have not been developed by the New England states—each state has defined status terms differently. Coded table entries must be used *for each state* as defined below. Table entries in parentheses are excerpted from the Nature Conservancy's New England Natural Heritage Program status list for amphibians and reptiles and can be used across New England.

The information provided in tables 1 and 2 is current as of March 1983. The list has been supplemented with additional state data obtained from revisions that have been made since the original publication date or that are currently in progress. Spaces are provided at the end of each table for the inclusion of other species.

Terms in the lists and abbreviations under the headings "SSAR" and "Federal List" in the two tables are defined by the Society for the Study of Amphibians and Reptiles—SSAR (Ashton 1976) and by the U.S. Department of the Interior, Fish and Wildlife Service (1980). Taxa are classified with respect to their status in each state. The state abbreviation precedes the classification on the table. Both the Department of the Interior and the SSAR list classifications for endangered (E) and threatened (T) taxa. (Of all the species considered here, the only one that is on the Federal list is the Plymouth redbelly turtle.) The SSAR further defines those species and subspecies that are rare (R) or peripheral (P).

Endangered (E): A taxon that has become reduced in numbers throughout its range (or has had its habitat reduced) to such a point that reproductive populations are extremely small or vulnerable to extirpation (SSAR). Those species in danger of extirpation throughout all or a significant part of their range (U.S. Dept. of Interior).

Threatened (T): A taxon that is represented in only a limited part of what was once its total range, with reduced populations due to habitat destruction or poor state or federal management (SSAR). Those species likely to become endangered within the foreseeable future throughout all or a significant portion of their range (U.S. Dept. of Interior).

Rare (R): Those species or subspecies that are considered rare throughout the state or are found in environmental conditions disjunct from the normal geographic range of the species (SSAR).

Peripheral (P): Those species or subspecies that reach the edge of their range in a state (SSAR).

The New England Natural Heritage Program of The Nature Conservancy has listed amphibians and reptiles in all the New England states according to their relative rarity and endangerment (1983). Species listings are based on guidelines that include limited range of individuals or breeding sites, and special factors that make a species particularly vulnerable to extirpation. These rankings are the most recent;

Northeastern Oak-Pine

Table 1. Amphibians with Special State Status in New England

Amphibian Species	SSAR	ME	NH	VT	MA	CT	RI
					State Lists		
Mudpuppy		(I)	R (I)	(S)	(I)	I (I)	I (I)
Marbled Salamander			U (SE)	(H)	SR, P* (ST)		S
Jefferson Salamander			R (ST)	(P)	SL, P* (P)		A
Silvery Salamander			(H)	(H)	(P)		
Blue-Spotted Salamander		(S)	(S)	(S)	SR, P* (P)	(SE)	A (H)
Tremblay's Salamander		(P)	(H)	(H)	(P)	(P)	(H)
Spotted Salamander					SLA, P*		S
Mountain Dusky Salamander				(H)		R	
Slimy Salamander			R (SE)	(H)	(H)	R (SE)	
Four-Toed Salamander		R 4 (ST)	R (ST)	(ST)	SLA, P* (ST)	I (ST)	S
Northern Spring Salamander		R 3	R		SLA, P* (ST)	R (ST)	A (H)
Eastern Spadefoot	CT(R)			(H)	P* (SE)	R (SE)	S (SE)
Fowler's Toad		(H)	(S)	(SE)			
Bullfrog					S*		
Mink Frog		(S)	(S)	(S)			
Northern Leopard Frog					P*	(S)	(H)

*Species status accompanied by protective legislation.

however, investigations on many of these species are ongoing (M. DesMeules, pers. comm.).

(T) Threatened throughout range and critically state endangered
(SE) State endangered
(ST) State threatened
(P) Possibly in peril, more information needed
(EX) Apparently extirpated from state
(H) Hypothetical occurrence from state
(I) Introduced species (nonnative)
(S) Apparently secure in the state, "watch" status may apply

The six states included in this program have agreed to protect all species that are federally listed. Further protection for amphibians and reptiles has been legislated in Massachusetts and Rhode Island at this writing. Lists of the less common species have been developed for Maine and Connecticut, but these

lists are unofficial and intended for future consideration. Legal status has not yet been provided. Vermont has not developed a listing of its herpetofauna.

In Maine, a listing prepared by the Critical Areas Program (Center for Natural Areas 1976) unofficially listed rare species for future consideration. Species were listed by a relative scarcity scale, R, of 1 to 4, common = 1, rare = 4.

New Hampshire has determined that no amphibian or reptile species are endangered or threatened—the two categories given legal protection by the state's Endangered Species Conservation Act, New Hampshire General Laws, Chapter 212-A, enacted in 1979. The state Fish and Game Department also lists species of concern, which includes eight R (rare) species of amphibians and

reptiles and three species with U (undetermined) status. There is no legislative protection for these categories.

In Massachusetts, certain species are legally protected by the Code of Massachusetts Regulations (321 CMR part 3.05), which authorizes the Division of Fish and Wildlife to promulgate regulations of Massachusetts General Laws Chapter 131, Section 5 (April 1980). These regulations rate species as P (protected) and S (season set for hunting or taking species).

Massachusetts also lists species that currently have no legal status (Massachusetts Division of Fisheries and Wildlife 1978). These are given three ratings:

E (endangered): Any species that is in danger of extinction through all or a significant portion of its range.

ST (state rare): Long-established breeding or wintering species quantitatively documented to be declining, facing extirpation from the Commonwealth, and considered likely to disappear without special action being taken.

SL (state local): Long-established breeding or wintering species in the Commonwealth that are restricted to very limited areas. A few species (SLA), which are widespread but nowhere frequent, are also included.

Connecticut species are unofficially listed for future consideration by Craig (1979). He creates five categories to designate the status of taxon in Connecticut, but only two classifications—"mode of occur-

rence" and "degree of threat"—are included in this book.

The following designations are furnished under "mode of occurrence—rarity":

R (rare): Small populations and or individuals are widespread in Connecticut but are limited in overall frequency of occurrence in relation to other animal taxa.

L (local): Taxa occur in only one or a few very restricted localities where, however, they may be abundant.

RL (rare and local): Individuals or small populations occur in one or a few highly restricted localities.

I (indeterminate): Sufficient data for determining the degree of rarity are not

available. Very secretive, poorly known taxa would fall into this category.

Under "degree of threat—endangerment" there are three groups:

V (vulnerable): Taxa that although not currently in danger of extinction (and whose numbers may even be stable or increasing) are nonetheless sufficiently rare to warrant concern. Their rarity may render them extremely vulnerable to unrestricted exploitation, unplanned development, or uncontrolled pollution.

T (state threatened): Taxa whose numbers have been undergoing a long-term, noncyclic decline in Connecticut. They are becoming depleted to the point where they are approaching "endan-

Table 2. Reptiles with Special State Status in New England

					State Lists			Federal
	SSAR	ME	NH	VT	MA	CT	RI	List
Stinkpot		R 4		(ST)				
Spotted Turtle		R 4 (ST)	(ST)	(H)	SL, P* (S)			
Bog Turtle	CT(E),RI(E)			(H)	SR, P* (H)	RL, T (SE)	A, P* (H)	
Wood Turtle		R 4 (S)	U (S)	(S)	SL, P* (S)		S, P*	
Eastern Box Turtle		R 4 (SE)	R (SE)	(H)	SLA, P* (ST)		P*	
Map Turtle				(S)				
Plymouth Redbelly Turtle	MA (R)				E, P* (T)			E*
Blanding's Turtle	ME(R), NH(R), MA(R)	R 4 (SE)	R (SE)	(H)	SL, P* (ST)	I, I (H)	A (H)	
Eastern Spiny Softshell				(P)				
Five-Lined Skink				(SE)	(EX)	RL, V (SE)	A	
Northern Brown Snake		R 3						
Northern Redbelly Snake						RL, V	S	
Eastern Ribbon Snake						(S)	S	
Eastern Hognose Snake			(SE)	(H)	P*		S	
Northern Ringneck Snake		R 3						
Eastern Worm Snake					SL, P* (ST)		S	
Eastern Smooth Green Snake						R, T	S	
Black Rat Snake		(EX)	R	(S)	P* (ST)	(S)	S	
Eastern Milk Snake		R 3						
Northern Copperhead					SR, P* (SE)		A (H)	
Timber Rattlesnake	CT(R),RI(E)	(EX)	U (SE)	(T)	SR, P* (SE)	RL, T (ST)	SE, P*	

*Species status accompanied by protective legislation.

gered" status. Natural or man-caused events may be responsible for their decline.

I (indeterminate): The degree of threat is unknown, due to a lack of information. Taxa that have recently colonized the state and about which little is known, obscure and secretive taxa, and taxa that have not been located in a number of years (although probably still present) might fall into this category.

The Rhode Island Department of Environmental Management, Division of Fish and Wildlife, provides legal protection of amphibian and reptile species, and lists as protected (P) those species protected under special rules and regulations provided in the state wildlife laws (Provision in Section 21-9 of the General Laws of the State of Rhode Island).

The Rhode Island Natural Heritage Program of 1980 developed an unofficial list of the species to be considered in planning: S (species for consideration): I (introduced species); A (species probably present in Rhode Island, although there are no verifiable records of their existence); SE (state endangered).*

Conservation

Amphibians and reptiles have suffered from habitat loss and degradation. Urbanization, draining and filling of wetlands, recreational development, water pollution, pesticides, and now acid precipitation are among the major factors exerting pressures on herpetofaunal habitats. In the past, bounty hunting extirpated the timber rattlesnake from parts of New England. Collection of specimens for biological supply houses has recently had adverse effects in some areas, especially on spotted salamanders and northern leopard frogs. Additional collecting for the pet trade and by hobbyists

has been excessive in some places, to the point where ambystomid breeding ponds and rattlesnake denning sites, for example, cannot be discussed freely. Some people keep live specimens. Unfortunately, collected individuals may not survive due to improper care; of those released, only those returned to the capture site have much chance of survival.

Many salamanders, frogs, and especially toads have an important role in insect predation; and many snakes help control rodent and insect populations. Since we know that the habitats of many of these species are diminishing both in availability and quality, it behooves all who are concerned about wildlife to become more familiar with amphibians and reptiles and their habitat needs. Efforts to coordinate systematic surveys to obtain distribution data, especially for salamanders, are just beginning. This information is essential to conservation efforts because, for many of these species, we just do not know what constitutes a viable population. We need information on breeding units and their distributions so that we can permit maintenance of gene flow throughout the population.

Observing amphibians and reptiles

Although they are abundant, most amphibians are not seen by the casual eye. Many remain motionless, their cryptic coloration rendering them quite "concealed." Basking turtles and water snakes dive into the water at a sudden noise or movement. A cautious approach while looking carefully is the rule. When out walking, turn logs, pieces of wood or bark, tin, or other debris to look for snakes or salamanders. Placing logs or old boards at marsh,

field, or wood edges may provide new shelters that can later be checked for occupants. In all cases, return overturned shelters to their original positions. Avoid destroying rotten logs or trees; they shelter a host of invertebrates and other organisms in addition to the amphibians and reptiles.

In spring, marshes and ponds should be visited in order to hear and observe breeding frogs and toads. Unless temperatures are too low, calls continue from late afternoon and through the night, until early the next morning. A headlamp, which leaves your hands free, or a flashlight, will enable you to find individuals, approach them carefully, and observe the performance close-up. Like spring peepers, salamanders are most easily observed at spring breeding ponds. Be prepared to visit roadside woodland ponds on the evenings of the first warm spring rains to observe the spectacular breeding congregations. If you capture individuals for examination, release them where you caught them. (The collection of specimens is restricted in many areas—check laws and local regulations before taking specimens.) Most people do not have adequate facilities for keeping specimens, which should be enjoyed in their native habitats. As Vogt (1981) suggests, take them home "only on film, tape, or as characteristic spots on your clothing"; we might add, "and as memories."

*The status of many species has changed among the New England states since 1983. For current information, contact the state agencies listed.

Checklist of New England Amphibians and Reptiles

Amphibia

CAUDATA

Necturidae
Mudpuppy   *Necturus m. maculosus*

Ambystomatidae
Marbled salamander   *Ambystoma opacum*
Jefferson salamander   *Ambystoma jeffersonianum*
Silvery salamander   *Ambystoma platineum*
Blue-spotted salamander   *Ambystoma laterale*
Tremblay's salamander   *Ambystoma tremblayi*
Spotted salamander   *Ambystoma maculatum*

Salamandridae
Red-spotted newt   *Notophthalmus v. viridescens*

Plethodontidae
Northern dusky salamander   *Desmognathus f. fuscus*
Mountain dusky salamander   *Desmognathus ochrophaeus*
Redback salamander   *Plethodon cinereus*
Slimy salamander   *Plethodon g. glutinosus*
Four-toed salamander   *Hemidactylium scutatum*
Northern spring salamander   *Gyrinophilus p. porphyriticus*
Northern two-lined salamander   *Eurycea b. bislineata*

ANURA

Pelobatidae
Eastern spadefoot   *Scaphiopus h. holbrookii*

Bufonidae
Eastern American toad   *Bufo a. americanus*
Fowler's toad   *Bufo woodhousii fowleri*

Hylidae
Northern spring peeper   *Hyla c. crucifer*
Gray treefrog   *Hyla versicolor*

Ranidae
Bullfrog   *Rana catesbeiana*
Green frog   *Rana clamitans melanota*
Mink frog   *Rana septentrionalis*
Wood frog   *Rana sylvatica*
Northern leopard frog   *Rana pipiens*
Pickerel frog   *Rana palustris*

Reptilia

TESTUDINES

Chelydridae
Common snapping turtle   *Chelydra s. serpentina*

Kinosternidae
Stinkpot   *Sternotherus odoratus*

Emydidae
Spotted turtle   *Clemmys guttata*
Bog turtle   *Clemmys muhlenbergii*
Wood turtle   *Clemmys insculpta*
Eastern box turtle   *Terrapene c. carolina*
Map turtle   *Graptemys geographica*
Red-eared slider   *Pseudemys scripta elegans*
Plymouth redbelly turtle   *Pseudemys rubriventris bangsi*
Eastern painted turtle   *Chrysemys p. picta*
Midland painted turtle   *Chrysemys picta marginata*
Blanding's turtle   *Emydoidea blandingii*

Trionychidae
Eastern spiny softshell   *Trionyx s. spiniferus*

SQUAMATA

LACERTILIA

Scincidae
Five-lined skink   *Eumeces fasciatus*

SERPENTES

Colubridae
Northern water snake   *Nerodia s. sipedon*
Northern brown snake   *Storeria d. dekayi*
Northern redbelly snake   *Storeria o. occipitomaculata*
Eastern garter snake   *Thamnophis s. sirtalis*
Maritime garter snake   *Thamnophis sirtalis pallidula*
Eastern ribbon snake   *Thamnophis s. sauritus*
Northern ribbon snake   *Thamnophis sauritus septentrionalis*
Eastern hognose snake   *Heterodon platyrhinos*
Northern ringneck snake   *Diadophis punctatus edwardsi*
Eastern worm snake   *Carphophis a. amoenus*
Northern black racer   *Coluber c. constrictor*
Eastern smooth green snake   *Opheodrys v. vernalis*
Black rat snake   *Elaphe o. obsoleta*
Eastern milk snake   *Lampropeltis t. triangulum*

Viperidae
Northern copperhead   *Agkistrodon contortrix mokeson*
Timber rattlesnake   *Crotalus horridus*

Salamanders

(order Caudata)

There are eight families of salamanders worldwide, and seven of them are represented by North American forms; of these, four occur in New England—the Necturidae, Ambystomatidae, Salamandridae, and Plethodontidae. New England is the northeastern range limit for four caudatans: the marbled *(Ambystoma opacum)*, slimy *(Plethodon g. glutinosus)*, silvery *(Ambystoma platineum)*, and Jefferson *(A. jeffersonianum)* salamanders. There are fifteen species of salamanders found in New England, if the mountain dusky salamander *(Desmognathus ochrophaeus)* is included (only one specimen, from Vermont, has been reported). The four species of the *Ambystoma jeffersonianum* complex have been treated separately. Although difficulties occur in distinguishing the triploids, *A. platineum* and *A. tremblayi,* without karyological and biochemical data, present research continues to add information on species distinction and evolution of this species complex.

Salamanders are typically nocturnal, secretive, and voiceless, and receive relatively little notice in comparison to that given to frogs and toads. Salamanders are amphibians and so have moist skin and lack external ear openings. Courtship involves chemoreception, rather than voice as in frogs and toads. All New England species fertilize their eggs internally without copulation. Males deposit spermatophores, pyramidal gelatinous structures capped with sperm packets. Females collect a sperm cap with their cloacal lips, and the eggs are fertilized as they pass through the cloaca. Most species lay their eggs in water. The aquatic larval stage ranges from a few months for the four-toed salamander *(Hemidactylium scutatum)* to four years for the northern spring salamander *(Gyrinophilus porphyriticus)*. The mudpuppy *(Necturus maculosus)* is the only truly neotenic New England species retaining gills throughout life. Only two New England species, the redback *(Plethodon cinereus)* and dusky *(Desmognathus f. fuscus)* salamanders, breed entirely terrestrially, selecting a moist cavity in or under a decaying log, or under stones or leaf litter (the latter species also uses caves). The larval stage of these two plethodons is completed before hatching.

The northern dusky salamander usually lays its eggs under stones, rotted logs, or other cover close to the water's edge. Upon hatching, the larvae move to the water where development continues.

Mudpuppy

Necturus m. maculosus
Caudata
Necturidae

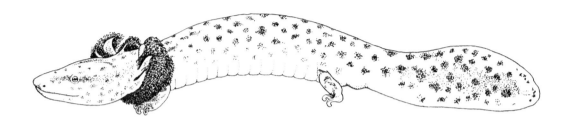

Range. St. Lawrence River west to
s.e. Manitoba, south to e. Kansas
and n. Alabama and through central
Pennsylvania to New York and the
Champlain Valley. Absent from the
Adirondacks. Introduced in parts of
New England.
Relative abundance. Uncommon.
Habitat. Entirely aquatic. Clear or
muddy waters of lakes, rivers,
ditches, large streams. One individual found at 90 ft (27.4 m) in Lake
Michigan (Behler and King
1979:283). Often found in and
around obstructions in streams and
in submerged log piles around the
bases of bridge pilings in larger
rivers (Shoop and Gunning 1967).
Special habitat requirements.
Moving water.
Age/size at sexual maturity. At 5 years
and at 8 in (20.3 cm) total length
(Bishop 1947:43). Retains external
gills as an adult.
Breeding period. Autumn (Bishop
1947:42).
Egg deposition. May and June of the
year following mating. Reproduces
in flowing water (Oliver 1955:211).
Prefers water depths of at least 3 ft

(0.9 m) and bottoms with weeds and
rocks to provide nesting cover. Nest
sites are often under large rock slabs
in water depths of 6 to 8 in (15 to 20
cm) in New York (Stewart 1961:68).
No. eggs/mass. 18 to 180 eggs (average 60 to 100) in water beneath objects, attached singly by stalks
(Bishop 1941:26).
Eggs hatch. 38 to 63 days, female
guards eggs (Bishop 1941:27).
Home range/movement. Displacement
of individuals in Louisiana suggests
homing ability. Occupy restricted
areas throughout the year (Shoop
and Gunning 1967).
Food habits/preferences. In New York,
aquatic insects comprised 30% of
the diet by weight, particularly
nymphs and larval forms, crustaceans, 33%, small fish, 13%, also
mollusks, spawn, other amphibians, worms, leeches and plants
(Hamilton 1932). Most food is captured at night along the bottom.
Comments. The mudpuppy is chiefly
nocturnal, bottom dwelling, and active through the winter, when it
moves to deeper water. This species
was first found in the Connecticut

River in Massachusetts in 1931
where laboratory specimens had
been released from Amherst College
(Warfel 1936). The Maine population also originated from released
individuals. The Rhode Island population origin is unknown, but is
presumed to be introduced as well
(Vinegar and Friedman 1967).
Selected references. Bishop 1947;
Logier 1952.

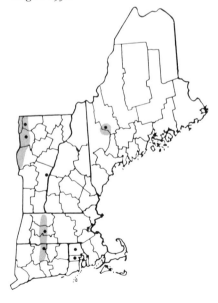

Marbled salamander

Ambystoma opacum
Caudata
Ambystomatidae

Range. Southern New Hampshire and central Massachusetts, central Pennsylvania west to s. Illinois, s. Missouri and e. Texas, south to n. Florida.

Relative abundance. Uncommon.

Habitat. Sandy and gravelly areas of mixed deciduous woodlands, especially oak-maple and oak-hickory (Minton 1972:46), trap rock slopes (M. Klemens, pers. commun.). During breeding season found in low areas around ponds, swamps, and quiet streams. Inhabits somewhat drier areas than other species of *Ambystoma*. During the summer usually found under logs and rocks. Found at 900 ft (274 m) above sea level in Connecticut (Babbitt 1937). Larvae usually found in temporary water throughout the winter. Probably hibernates in deep burrows.

Special habitat requirements. Ponds or swamps in wooded areas for breeding.

Age/size at sexual maturity. 15 to 18 months.

Breeding period and egg deposition. During the fall, adults migrate to breeding areas (September in the northern parts of range) (Bishop 1941:138).

No. eggs/mass. 50 to 232 (average 100) eggs laid singly in shallow depressions beneath surface materials (Bishop 1941:142). Eggs laid in dry beds of temporary ponds and streams or at the edge of ponds or swamps, where they will be washed into the water to hatch.

Time to hatching. 15 to 207 days; female forms a nest site and may brood eggs (Oliver 1955:234).

Eggs hatch. Usually in fall or early winter when submerged; without rain, will hatch in spring.

Larval period. Larvae overwinter with little growth until spring, and transform to terrestrial form in late May to June (Noble and Brady 1933). A higher temperature and abundant food supply will hasten metamorphosis (Stewart 1956b). The larval period was 135 days in New Jersey (Hassinger et al. 1970).

Home range/movement. Adults migrate an average of 194 m from breeding sites to summer range in Indiana (Williams 1973 cited in Semlitsch 1980b:320).

Food habits/preferences. Arthropods, including adults and larval insects, and crustaceans. Also takes earthworms and mollusks. Marbled salamander larvae eat small aquatic insects, crustaceans, and other small

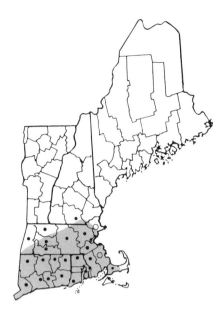

invertebrates, and are cannibalistic (Minton 1972:47). Larvae rise in the water column to feed (T. Tyning, pers. commun.).

Comments. Terrestrial and nocturnal, often using runways of other animals or tunnels through loose soil. Young larvae are aquatic and primarily nocturnal.

Selected references. Bishop 1941; Anderson 1967b; Hassinger et al. 1970; Lazell 1979.

Jefferson salamander

Ambystoma jeffersonianum
Caudata
Ambystomatidae

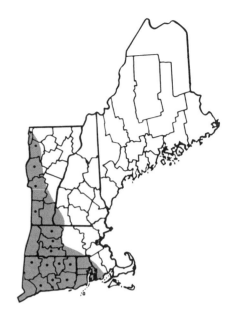

Range. Western New England to w. central Indiana, central Kentucky to central Virginia and north to n. New Jersey.

Relative abundance. Locally common to rare.

Habitat. Undisturbed damp, shady deciduous or mixed woods, bottom-lands, swamps, ravines, moist pastures, or lake shores. Terrestrial, it hides beneath leaf litter, under stones, or in decomposing logs and stumps. Cleared strips create a barrier for dispersal (Pough and Wilson 1976). Hardwood forests on glaciated limestone areas northwest of the Great Swamp in New Jersey (Anderson and Giacosie 1967). In Connecticut, members of the *Ambystoma jeffersonianum* complex are more abundant and widespread in upland areas of the Connecticut and Housatonic river valleys (M. Klemens, pers. commun.) and have been documented within shale ravines in Connecticut (Babbitt 1937). Hibernates on land in winter months, usually near breeding waters. Have been found within rotten logs.

Special habitat requirements. Requires temporary ponds for breeding period.

Age/size at sexual maturity. Females at 21 months (Bishop 1941:102); snout to vent length 70 to 75 mm males, 75 to 80 mm females (Minton 1954). Juveniles probably enter the breeding population at 2 to 3 years of age (Wilson 1976 cited in Thompson et al. 1980:119).

Breeding period and egg deposition. February to April, migrates to ponds and vernal pools (Brandon 1961). Breeds earlier than *A. maculatum* in central Pennsylvania (Gatz 1971). Eggs are deposited, often beneath ice. Will tolerate pH of 4 to 8, with best hatching success at 5 to 6 pH range (Pough and Wilson 1976). Isolated upland pools bordered by shrubs and surrounded by forest were primary breeding sites in Maryland (Thompson et al. 1980). Temporary ponds frequently used as breeding sites.

No. eggs/mass. 107 to 286 eggs (Oliver 1955:234). Many variations of egg deposition, laid singly or in small cylindrical masses of 1 to 35 eggs each, in water attached to twigs or plants or under rocks. Egg masses average 16 eggs per mass (Bishop 1941:94).

Eggs hatch. 30 to 45 days (Bishop 1947:135). 13 to 45 days (Oliver 1955:234).

Larval period. 56 to 125 days (Bishop 1941:99).

Home range/movement. Adults migrated an average of 252 m from breeding ponds to summer range in Indiana. Newly metamorphosized individuals moved an average 92 m from the ponds (Williams 1973 cited in Semlitsch 1980b:320). In hardwood forest of n. Kentucky, adults moved an average of 250 m from ponds in a series of 6 to 8 moves in 45 days (Douglas and Monroe 1981).

Food habits/preferences. Small invertebrates, including worms, millipedes, spiders, insects, and aquatic crustaceans. Feeds on most animal life that it can capture. Larvae are cannibalistic.

Selected references. Anderson and Giacosie 1967; Uzzell 1967a; Pough and Wilson 1976.

Silvery salamander
Ambystoma platineum
Caudata
Ambystomatidae

Range. Occurs with *A. jeffersonianum*; however, range is mainly restricted to areas north of the Wisconsin glacial moraine where ranges of *A. jeffersonianum* and *A. laterale* meet or overlap. Central Indiana east to n. New Jersey and w. Massachusetts.
Relative abundance. Locally common–rare.
Habitat. Found with *A. jeffersonianum* in hardwood forests in Sussex Co., New Jersey (Anderson and Giacosie 1967).
Special habitat requirements. See *A. jeffersonianum.*
Age/size at sexual maturity. Unreported.
Breeding period and egg deposition. Breeds from March to April (Behler and King 1979:296).
No. eggs/mass. Typically 15 to 20 eggs/mass, in cylindrical masses attached to submerged twigs and grass stems. Rarely if ever attached to pond-bottom debris (Uzzell 1967c:49.1).
Home range/movement. Unreported.

Food habits/preferences. Unreported.
Comments. A hybrid of Jefferson and blue-spotted salamanders with 3 sets of chromosomes (2 sets from *A. jeffersonianum* and 1 from *A. laterale*). Most are female, only one male has been recorded (Smith 1978:88). Genetic material is not contributed by male *A. jeffersonianum*; the sperm only stimulates egg production (Uzzell 1964). *A. jeffersonianum* and *A. laterale* probably developed from a common ancestor that was reproductively isolated by the Wisconsin glaciation, and as the glacier retreated, the two species mixed and hybridization occurred (Uzzell 1964).

All four species of the complex have been found to occur sympatrically in a few areas; *A. laterale* and *A. tremblayi* are generally more northern, *A. jeffersonianum* and *A. platineum* are generally more southern in the range of the complex (Austin and Bogart 1982).

Preserved male specimens identi-fied as *A. platineum* are most likely *A. jeffersonianum* (Uzzell 1967c:49.2).
Selected references. Uzzell 1964, 1967c; Smith 1978.

Blue-spotted salamander
Ambystoma laterale
Caudata
Ambystomatidae

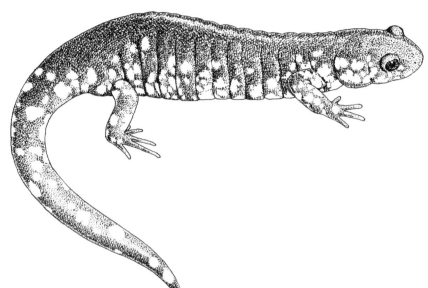

Range. Southeastern Quebec and the n. shore of the Gulf of St. Lawrence to James Bay and the s. end of Lake Winnipeg, south to n. Illinois and Indiana, n. New York and New England. Disjunct colonies in New Jersey, Long Island, Iowa, and Labrador.

Relative abundance. Rare; threatened in southern portion of range.

Habitat. Wooded, swampy, or moist areas (Minton 1954). Occasionally overgrown pastures. Sometimes occurs where soil is sandy, and may be found under logs or other forest debris. In hardwood forests in the remnants of glacial lake Passaic in New Jersey (Anderson and Giacosie 1967). Occurs in a wide range of elevations (in w. Connecticut) and along the Connecticut River flood plain (M. Klemens, pers. commun.).

Special habitat requirements. Ponds or semipermanent water for breeding.

Age/size at sexual maturity. Snout to vent length of 47 to 55 mm in Indiana (Minton 1954).

Breeding period and egg deposition. Breeds during early spring rains when night temperatures are above freezing (Lazell 1968). Eggs laid, March to early April, on the bottoms of temporary shallow forest ponds, roadside drainage ditches, temporary pasture ponds, kettle holes (Landre 1980), in small pools of bogs (Bleakney 1957), attached to litter or in bottom detritus (Stille 1954), and twigs (Uzzell 1967b:48.1).

No. eggs/mass. 199 to 247 eggs (Uzzell 1964); 82 to 489 eggs (Minton 1972:36). Often laid singly (Uzzell 1967b); 6 to 10 eggs per mass (Landre 1980).

Eggs hatch. About 1 month (Smith 1961:28).

Larval period. Extending to late June or mid-August (Smith 1961:28). Found overwintering in Nova Scotia (Bleakney 1952).

Home range/movement. Unreported.

Food habits/preferences. Arthropods, annelids, and centipedes.

Comments. Acid precipitation and habitat loss are major threats to this species in the Northeast.

Selected references. Anderson and Giacosie 1967; Uzzell 1964, 1967b; Landre 1980.

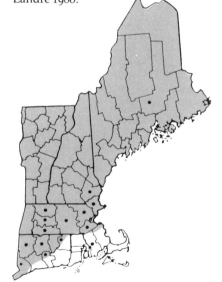

Tremblay's salamander
Ambystoma tremblayi
Caudata
Ambystomatidae

Range. Disjunct colonies in New Brunswick, Ottawa River drainage, e. Massachusetts, New Jersey, n.w. Ohio, Indiana, and Michigan, and n. Wisconsin.

Relative abundance. Rare.

Habitat. Deciduous forests surrounding small ponds or lakes (Minton 1972:37). Has been found under logs.

Special habitat requirements. Woodland ponds for breeding.

Age/size at sexual maturity. Unreported.

Breeding period and egg deposition. In early spring, migrates to breeding ponds; egg deposition March to April (Minton 1972:38; Uzzell 1964).

No. eggs/mass. 135 to 162 eggs (Uzzell 1964), laid in groups of 2, 3, or 4, sometimes singly, in small clusters at pond bottoms or attached to submerged sticks (Uzzell 1967d:50.1).

Eggs hatch. Unreported.

Larval period. Transforms in 95 to 101 days (Uzzell 1964). Larval period shortens as eggs are deposited later in the spring.

Home range/movement. Unreported.

Food habits/preferences. Thought to be similar to *A. laterale.*

Comments. Tremblay's salamander is a triploid of hybrid origin from *A. laterale* and *A. jeffersonianum*. It is morphologically similar to *A. laterale,* from which it receives 2 sets of chromosomes; only 1 set is contributed by *A. jeffersonianum*. The population consists of females only (gynogenetic reproduction), and depends upon males of *A. laterale* to stimulate egg development (Uzzell 1964). The spermatophore of *A. laterale* is picked up but the sperm does not penetrate the egg.

Electrophoretic analyses of protein sera continue to add new information on the genetic origins and distributions of members of this species complex.

Spotted salamander
Ambystoma maculatum
Caudata
Ambystomatidae

Range. Nova Scotia and the Gaspé Peninsula to s. Ontario, throughout New England, south through Wisconsin, s. Illinois excluding prairie regions, to e. Kansas and Texas, and through the e. United States, except Florida, the Delmarva Peninsula and s. New Jersey.

Relative abundance. Common, although populations declining, possibly due to acid precipitation and over-collection.

Habitat. Moist woods, streambanks, beneath stones, logs, boards. Fossorial, it prefers deciduous or mixed woods on rocky hillsides and shallow woodland ponds or marshy pools that hold water through the summer for breeding. Usually does not breed in ponds containing fish (Anderson 1967a). Terrestrial hibernator. In summer often wanders far from water source. Found in low oak-hickory forests with creeks and nearby swamps in Illinois (Cagle 1942 cited in Smith 1961:30). Has been found in the pitch-pine–scrub-oak community of the Albany Pine Bush (Stewart and Rossi 1981), dense oak forests in Rhode Island.

Special habitat requirements. Mesic woods with semipermanent water for breeding. Eggs tolerate pH range of 6 to 10 with best hatching success at pH of 7 to 9 (Pough and Wilson 1976). High embryonic mortality occurred in temporary pools with pH below 6 in New York (Pough 1976).

Age/size at sexual maturity. During second year. Males may mature 1 year earlier than females (Wacasey 1961).

Breeding period and egg deposition. Breeds from March to mid-April.

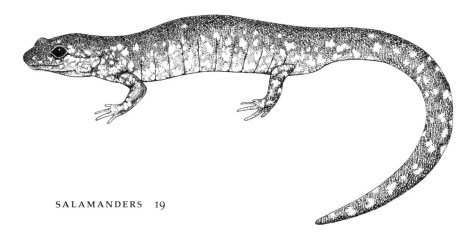

Mass breeding migrations occur in this species; individuals enter and leave breeding ponds using the same track each year, and exhibit fidelity to breeding ponds (Shoop 1965, 1968, 1974). Individuals may not breed in consecutive years (Husting 1965). Breeding migrations occur during steady evening rainstorms. Eggs are deposited 1 to 6 days after first appearance of adults at ponds (Bishop 1941:114).

No. eggs/mass. 100 to 200 eggs, average of 125, laid in large masses of jelly, sometimes milky, attached to stems about 15 cm under water. Each female lays 1 to 10 masses (average of 2 to 3) of eggs (Wright and Allen 1909). Woodward (1982) found females breeding in permanent ponds produced smaller, more numerous eggs than females breeding in temporary ponds.

Eggs hatch. 31 to 54 days (Bishop 1947:145). In a cold (≤10C) spring-fed pond, eggs developed in 60 days in Rhode Island (Whitford and Vinegar 1966); Shoop (1974) reported 8 to 14 days.

Larval period. 61 to 110 days, 15 to 60 days (Shoop 1974), found overwintering in Nova Scotia (Bleakney 1952) and Rhode Island (Whitford and Vinegar 1966). Transforms July to September.

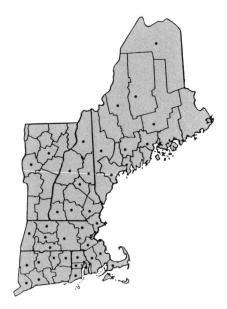

Home range/movement. Individuals have been found up to ¼ mi (400 m) from the nearest breeding site in North Carolina (Gordon 1968). Will travel 100 to 200 yd (91 to 182 m) from woods to ponds in open meadows in New York (M. Stewart, pers. commun.). Individuals were found to use subterranean rodent burrows as retreats; tagged salamanders that were monitored were found within a 300 cm² area of these burrows. Displaced adults moved up to 500 m to return to breeding ponds in Massachusetts (Shoop 1968). Average migration of 150 m from breeding

ponds in Kentucky (6 to 220 m range) in thick oak-hickory forest. Linear migration was unaffected by the presence or absence of vegetation or change in the topography (Douglas and Monroe 1981). Adults' rate of movement during breeding migrations ranged from 6 to 11 m/hr (Whitford and Vinegar 1966).

Food habits/preferences. Earthworms, snails, slugs, insects, spiders, particularly larval and adult beetles (Wacasey 1961). Larval stage may also eat small fish. Cannibalism by larvae occurs under crowded conditions.

Comments. Nocturnal; found above ground only during migrations to and from breeding pools. Rainfall, snowmelt, or high humidity coupled with air temperature of 10C or more are necessary for migrations to breeding pools.

Selected references. Shoop 1965; Anderson 1967a; Douglas and Monroe 1981.

Red-spotted newt
Notophthalmus v. viridescens
Caudata
Salamandridae

Range. Nova Scotia and the Gaspé Peninsula west to the n. shore of Lake Superior and e. Michigan south throughout New England to central Alabama, n. central Georgia. Absent along coast from s.e. South Carolina, southward.

Relative abundance. Common to abundant.

Habitat. Adults found in ponds, particularly water with abundant submerged vegetation, and in weedy areas of lakes, marshes, ditches, backwaters, and pools of shallow slow-moving streams or other unpolluted shallow or semipermanent

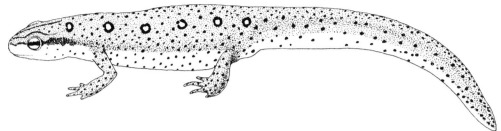

water. Terrestrial juveniles (efts) live in moist areas, typically under damp leaves, under brush piles or logs and stumps, usually in wooded habitats. More common in areas of higher elevation in Connecticut (M. Klemens, pers. commun.); from sea level to 1.6 km elevation on Mt. Marcy in the Adirondacks (M. Stewart, pers. observ.). Moist beech-maple-hemlock woods in New York (Hurlbert 1969), and oak-pine woods in Massachusetts (Healy 1974). May be seen moving about on wet days in spring and summer. Efts hibernate on land, burrowing under logs and debris, but most adults remain active all winter underwater in pond bottoms or in streams. During winter months often found semiactive in groups of 20 to 40 (Morgan and Grierson 1932).

Special habitat requirements. Water with aquatic vegetation for the adult newt.

Age/size at sexual maturity. 2 to 8 years (Healy 1974). Aquatic juveniles feed almost year round and mature in 2 years. The eft feeds only during rainy summer periods and requires a longer time to reach maturity.

Breeding period and egg deposition. Spring (April to June), fall (August to October), sometimes November to December (Hurlbert 1969). Characteristically breed in lakes, ponds, and swamps (Hurlbert 1970).

No. eggs/mass. 200 to 375 eggs (Bishop 1941:64), laid in water, attached singly to the leaves of aquatic plants.

Eggs hatch. 3 to 5 weeks (Logier 1952:64), temperature dependent.

Larval period. 12 to 16 weeks. Post-larval migration from aquatic to terrestrial habitat occurs from summer through late fall during diurnal rainfall in New York (Hurlbert 1970).

Home range/movement. Approximately 270 m² for red efts (juveniles) in an oak-pine woodland in w. Massachusetts; maximum daily movement was 13 m (Healy 1974). Average movement along the edge of a small pond in Pennsylvania was 10.1 ft (3.1 m) for females, and 11.2 ft (3.4 m) for males; most individuals remained within 5 ft (1.5 m) of shore (Bellis 1968). Harris (1981) found all movement was random for 323 males in a pond in Virginia, dismissing the concept of home range or territoriality for males.

Food habits/preferences. Both adults and larvae are opportunistic feeders (Burton 1977). Insects and their larvae, particularly mayfly, caddisfly, midge and mosquito larvae (Ries and Bellis 1966), springtails (MacNamara 1977); tadpoles, frog eggs, worms, leeches, small mollusks and crustaceans, spiders, mites, occasionally small minnows (Hamilton 1932); salamander eggs also a major food item (T. Tyning, pers. commun.). Also ingests molted skin. Snails are an important food source

for the red eft (Burton 1976). Adult cannibalism on own larvae provides an important component of the diet in July and August (Burton 1977).

Comments. Mates in ponds and streams. The red eft remains on land for 2 to 7 years; most remain on land 4 to 5 years, then return to the water where they transform to aquatic adults (Healy 1974). Neotenic individuals have been found on the Coastal Plain in Massachusetts, New York (Bishop 1941:73–75), and Rhode Island (S. Nyman, pers. commun.). Some individual populations omit the terrestrial eft stage. Skin secretions of red efts are highly toxic—about 10 times more toxic than those of adults (Brodie 1968).

Selected references. Bishop 1947; Mecham 1967.

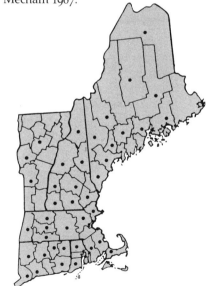

Northern dusky salamander

Desmognathus f. fuscus
Caudata
Plethodontidae

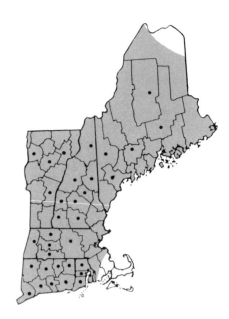

Range. Southern New Brunswick and s. Quebec to s.e. Indiana and central Kentucky to the Carolinas; throughout the Northeast excluding s. New Jersey.

Relative abundance. Common to abundant.

Habitat. Woodlands at the margins of cool running water; clear rocky streams; spring edges, seepage areas, beds of semidry brooks; under cover of wet leaves, moss, rock piles, other debris, or in burrows in the soil. It ventures from streamside only during wet weather. Occurs from sea level to mountain elevations. Moves under logs and rocks in deeper water to hibernate in September. May remain active throughout the winter in stream bottoms or deep in unfrozen soil (Ashton and Ashton 1978). Formerly found in bluffs overlooking the Harlem River in Manhattan (Gans 1945).

Special habitat requirements. Permanent streams or seeps in woodlands.

Age/size at sexual maturity. About 3 years (Dunn 1926:92); males at 3½ years, females deposit first eggs at 5 years (Organ 1961). Males mature at 2 years, females at 3 years (Danstedt 1975). Body size at maturity varies between populations (Tilley 1968).

Breeding period and egg deposition. Breeding occurs in either fall or spring (Bishop 1941:312–13). Evidence for biennial breeding cycle in females (Organ 1961). Breeds in ponds or streams. Eggs are deposited from June to September in Connecticut (Babbitt 1937). Female guards the eggs in damp hollows beneath stones, under loose bark of logs, between wet leaf litter layers, and in moss close to the water's edge. Larvae move to water where development continues (M. Stewart, pers. commun.). Clutches found less than 50 cm from the edge of streams and springs or in seepage areas (Krysik 1980).

No. eggs/mass. 8 to 28 stalked eggs in compact clusters, average 17 (Bishop 1941:314).

Eggs hatch. 7 to 8 weeks in Massachusetts (Wilder 1917); 5 to 8 weeks in New York (Bishop 1941:318); about 10 weeks in Connecticut (Babbitt 1937:16).

Larval period. 7 to 10 months, usually transform in June (Wilder 1913:295). From 9 to 12 months in Maryland (Danstedt 1975).

Home range/movement. Less than 10 ft (3 m) along a stream in a wooded ravine in Pennsylvania (Barthalmus and Bellis 1969). Average range of 1.4 m² in a gravel-bottom stream in Ohio (Ashton and Ashton 1978). Average about 150 ft² (14 m²) along a stream in Kentucky, maximum movement of 100 ft (30.5 m) as open water dried up (Barbour 1971:57). Average weekly movement less than 0.5 m (Ashton 1975). In an intermittent mountain stream average for 5 individuals was 48 m², daily movements less than 2 m (Barbour et al. 1969a).

Food habits/preferences. Small aquatic and terrestrial invertebrates, insects to 96% of prey by weight (Burton 1976), grubs, worms, crustaceans, spiders, and occasionally mollusks; sometimes larvae of own species. Nocturnal feeder, also active on cloudy or rainy days.

Comments. Larval stage is aquatic, adults are riparian. Kieran (1959:139) believed this species to be the most common salamander within New York City limits.

Selected references. Bishop 1947; Organ 1961; Ashton 1975.

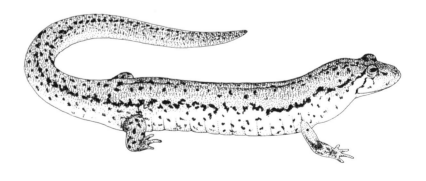

Mountain dusky salamander

Desmognathus ochrophaeus
Caudata
Plethodontidae

Range. Appalachian mountains and uplands from New York to n. Georgia at altitudes ranging from a few hundred feet (approx. 60 m) above sea level to timberline in the s. Appalachians. One unconfirmed juvenile specimen from central Vermont (Lazell 1976b).

Relative abundance. Rare.

Habitat. Stream edges and forest floor. In wet woods under forest debris, logs, stones, sometimes beneath the bark of dead trees. Near water—small streams, springs, or seeps. Seeps and springs used for late autumn and winter hibernation. Individuals inhabiting seepage banks are active earlier in spring and later in the fall than streamside individuals (Keen 1979).

Special habitat requirements. Semiterrestrial, it requires seeps, springs, or streams in woodland areas.

Age/size at sexual maturity. About 3 years: females at 36 months deposit clutch at 30 to 34 mm snout-vent length (Keen and Orr 1980).

Breeding period and egg deposition. Late winter/spring or autumn (Fitz-patrick 1973). Female guards eggs.

No. eggs/mass. 11 to 14 eggs (Bishop 1941:335). Stalked eggs deposited in clusters underneath stones or logs in small cavities. Fecundity in *Desmognathus* is size dependent (Tilley 1968).

Eggs hatch. 50 to 70 days (Tilley 1972), hatching in fall and early spring.

Larval period. 2 to 8 months (Tilley 1970); in the s. Appalachians, larvae occasionally overwinter (Tilley 1973:129.1).

Home range/movement. Average movement of 40 to 45 cm beween captures of displaced and nondisplaced individuals in a rock-face habitat in North Carolina (Huheey and Brandon 1973). Homing to the nest shown by breeding females (Forester 1979). Females are philopatric, ovipositing in the same section of a stream in successive years (Forester 1977).

Food habits/preferences. Insects, including adult and larval forms of flies, beetles, wasps, ants, and segmented worms (Keen 1979), also takes other small arthropods (Huheey and Brandon 1973). Eats shed skin (Bishop 1941:341).

Comments. Basically nocturnal but also active on dark humid days. Will climb trees and shrubs to feed.

Selected references. Bishop 1947; Hairston 1949; Huheey and Brandon 1973; Tilley 1973.

Redback salamander

Plethodon cinereus
Caudata
Plethodontidae

Range. Nova Scotia throughout New England, west to s. Ontario and e. Minnesota, south in scattered colonies to Missouri, in the Smoky Mountains, in s. Tennessee and east to Cape Hatteras.

Relative abundance. Abundant.

Habitat. Mixed deciduous or coniferous woods. Entirely terrestrial, it inhabits interiors of decaying logs and stumps, also found underneath stones, moist leaf litter, and bark. Wet areas and extremely moist bottomland avoided. Enters xeric, sandy habitats where moist microhabitats exist (M. Klemens, pers. commun.).

Hibernates at 15 in (38 cm) soil depth (Oliver 1955:121) or in rock crevices. May be active during mild winter weather (Minton 1972:67). In Indiana, individuals were found active in an ant mound throughout the winter (Caldwell 1975). Found hibernating 30 to 36 in (76.2 to 91.4 cm) deep in decaying root systems of dead white oaks in s.e. Massachusetts (Hoff 1977). Has been found hibernating in aquatic situations in Maryland (Cooper 1956).

Special habitat requirements. Logs, stumps, rocks, etc.

Age/size at sexual maturity. Generally during second year (Oliver 1955:277), but female usually reproduces in third year (Burger 1935).

Breeding period and egg deposition. Eggs are deposited from June to September.

No. eggs/mass. 3 to 14 eggs, average 7 to 10, in small clusters attached to roof of small chamber, laid in and under rotted logs and stumps. Reproduces annually in Connecticut (Lotter 1978).

Eggs hatch. 30 to 60 days (Oliver 1955:234), extending to 84 days in Maine (Banasiak 1974). Hatch in August to September. Larval stage is completed within egg.

Home range/movement. Home range is small due to restricted horizontal movements (Taub 1961). Movement of less than 1 ft (30.5 cm) for 14 individuals in hardwood forest habitat in New Jersey; individuals usually found under the same object where initially captured (Taub 1961). Home ranges of 13 m² for females, about 24 m² for males were determined in a northern hardwood forest in Michigan (Kleeberger and Werner 1982).

Food habits/preferences. Small insects and their larvae, earthworms, snails, slugs, spiders, sowbugs, millipedes, mites (Surface 1913:95). Occasionally cannibalistic. Mites were the most important food, comprising 65% of the prey items in a New Hampshire study (Burton 1976); insects, 73% by weight in a New York study (Jameson 1944). During rainy summer nights found on leaf litter presumably foraging for food (Burton and Likens 1975). Often climbs tree trunks and shrubs in search of food, particularly during wet nights.

Comments. Three distinct color phases occur: redback, leadback, and erythristic. In Connecticut, the

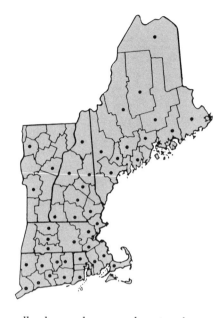

redback morph occurs almost exclusively in cold upland areas; in areas of more moderate climate and elevation, both redback and leadback morphs occur (M. Klemens, pers. commun.). All records of erythristic individuals occur north of 41° and south of 47° latitude (Tilley et al. 1982). The redback salamander is the most abundant terrestrial vertebrate in New England and comprises the greatest amount of vertebrate biomass in the Hubbard Brook Experimental Forest in New Hampshire (Burton and Likens 1975).

Selected references. Heatwole 1962; Smith 1963.

Slimy salamander

Plethodon g. glutinosus
Caudata
Plethodontidae

Range. Extreme w. Connecticut through central New York to e. Oklahoma, Arkansas, south in Louisiana to central Florida. Scattered colonies in s. New Hampshire and Texas.

Relative abundance. Uncommon to rare.

Habitat. Moist wooded hillsides and ravines. Terrestrial, it is found underneath moist humus, manure piles, in crevices in rocks, shale banks, and under logs in woodland areas. Bishop (1941:228) found the species most abundant in banks along highways and woodland openings. Has been found in second-growth oak-hickory forests and steep hemlock slopes of ravines in the Helderberg Mountains, New York (M. Stewart, pers. commun.); also in mature mixed deciduous forests (Semlitsch 1980a). Hibernates underground from November to March or April.

Special habitat requirements. Rock outcroppings, logs within wooded areas.

Age/size at sexual maturity. Females mature at about 4 years and lay eggs in the fifth year, males at 4 years (Highton 1962). Lengths of 59 to 74 mm snout to vent length in females, 53 to 70 mm in males (Highton 1962).

Breeding period and egg deposition. Breeds in autumn and spring (Highton 1956). Probable biennial oviposition occurring in late spring or early summer in northern populations (Highton 1962). Eggs laid within rock crevices or rotted logs (Smith 1961:58), also found in caves (Bishop 1941:224).

No. eggs/mass. 13 to 34 eggs, average 16 to 17 (Highton 1962). Eggs aggregated in a thin envelopment. Fecundity increases with body size (Semlitsch 1980a).

Eggs hatch. Probably in late summer; entire larval period spent within egg.

Home range/movement. Twenty-two individuals in n. Florida were recaptured at or within 4 ft (1.2 m) of the original capture point (Highton 1956). Adult home ranges less than 9 m diameter, immatures less than 6 m diameter, in oak-hickory forest with thick leaf litter in North Carolina. Mean movement distances were 17.5 m for males, 14.3 m for females, and 4.2 m for juveniles. Probably capable of movements over 90 m beyond home range area (Wells and Wells 1976).

Food habits/preferences. Euryphagic (Powders and Tietjen 1974). Mostly insects; also sowbugs, worms, centipedes, spiders, slugs, and snails (Hamilton 1932). Availability probably governs feeding habits. Ants and beetles were the most abundant food items in a Virginia study, comprising 58% of the total weight of food (Davidson 1956).

Comments. Nocturnal, may be active during some rainy days. During hot dry spells found deep underground or under logs in dense aggregations (Wells and Wells 1976).

Selected references. Bishop 1941; Highton 1956, 1962.

Four-toed salamander

Hemidactylium scutatum
Caudata
Plethodontidae

Range. Nova Scotia west to s. Ontario and Wisconsin, south to Alabama and Georgia. Absent from most of n. New England. Disjunct populations occur in Maine.

Relative abundance. Uncommon to rare.

Habitat. Wet woodlands, preferably with sphagnum moss; shaded, shallow woodland pools; tamarack bogs. Hides in moss, in moist decaying wood, under stones or wet leaves. Prefers an acidic environment. Found in beech-maple, yellow birch-maple and other hardwood forests, found less often in coniferous woods (Neill 1963:2.1). In mixed forests in New York (Bishop 1941:190). Maple, alder sapling swamp in Connecticut (C. Raithel, pers. commun.). Larval stage is aquatic, found in pools and quiet streams with an abundance of moss. Typically hibernates in decaying root systems of trees. Aggregations may appear during hibernation within rotted wood or leaf litter (Blanchard 1933b).

Special habitat requirements. Acidic wet woodlands.

Age/size at sexual maturity. About 2½ years (Barbour 1971:74).

Breeding period and egg deposition. Breeds in late summer and autumn, peaks in fall. Breeding area adjacent to mixed hardwood or northern conifer woods in West Virginia (N. Green, pers. observ.), Albany County, New York (M. Stewart, pers. commun.), and Michigan (Blanchard 1923). Eggs are deposited the next spring— March to April or May (Blanchard 1934, Barbour 1971:73). Eggs laid singly; adhered to moss, in natural cavities or in depressions formed by the female over or adjacent to water, usually in sphagnum but also among roots, decayed leaves. When the larvae hatch, they drop into the water below.

No. eggs/mass. 19 to 50 eggs (Dunn 1926:200, 202), average 50 in New York (Bishop 1941:183). Communal nesting may occur with up to 800 eggs laid per nest. One to four females will remain with eggs (Wood 1953).

Eggs hatch. 38 to 60 days (Blanchard 1934).

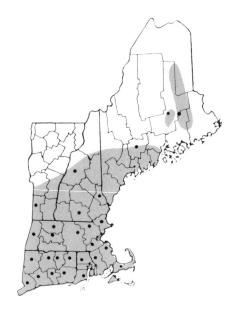

Larval period. 6 weeks (Blanchard 1923) to 18 weeks; variation in larval development time is dependent upon pond conditions (Bishop 1941:186).

Home range/movement. Unreported.

Food habits/preferences. Small invertebrates, including insects, spiders, earthworms.

Comments. A nocturnal and secretive species, therefore difficult to locate.

Selected references. Bishop 1947; Neill 1963.

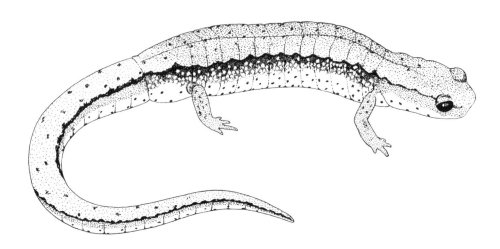

Northern spring salamander

Gyrinophilus p. porphyriticus
Caudata
Plethodontidae

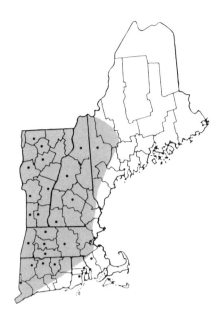

Range. Through the Appalachian range from w. central Maine and extreme s.e. Quebec south to e. Ohio and central Alabama, Pennsylvania, and n. New Jersey. Absent from the Coastal Plain.

Relative abundance. Uncommon to rare, except in Vermont and n.w. Berkshire County, Massachusetts, where common (T. Tyning, pers. commun.).

Habitat. Found in but not restricted to forested areas with clear cold water, springs, mountain streams, creeks, boggy areas. Also in depressions under stones or other cover adjacent to water. Usually occurs at higher elevations in spruce-fir forests, typically in moist situations, in underground water courses, and limestone caves (N. Green, pers. observ.), beech-maple-hemlock forests, in shale ravine streams in Tompkins and Albany counties, New York (M. Stewart, pers. commun.). Has been found in hillside meadow streams, swamps, and lake margins.

Special habitat requirements. Streams, seeps, or springs. In winter, wet soil near water, where it remains somewhat active in burrows.

Age/size at sexual maturity. 4 to 5 years, at total length of about 5½ in (14 cm) in New York (Bishop 1947:370).

Breeding period and egg deposition. Breeds from mid-October to winter months (Bruce 1972). Annual reproduction cycle (Bruce 1969). Eggs deposited from April to summer and into the fall (Bruce 1972), female guards eggs (Organ 1961).

No. eggs/mass. 9 to 63 eggs (Bruce 1972); 44 to 132 eggs (Bishop 1941:247); 44 to 66 eggs (Organ 1961). Eggs laid in running water under logs and stones, usually in groups, sometimes attached singly.

Eggs hatch. Hatch late summer. Early fall (Organ 1961). The young from one clutch may remain near the nest site for several months after hatching (Bruce 1980).

Larval period. Variable larval period, average about 4 years. Metamorphosis occurs in late spring and summer (Bruce 1980). Larvae are aquatic.

Home range/movement. Unreported.

Food habits/preferences. Euryphagic predators—consume aquatic insects and their nymph and larval forms, crustaceans, centipedes, earthworms, snails, spiders, millipedes, small frogs, and salamanders. Terrestrial insects were 79% of total prey items in New Hampshire (Burton 1976). Has been found to eat its own larvae (Logier 1952:76). Salamanders comprise 50% of the diet in the Appalachians (Bruce 1972); but are a minor part of diet in New York (Bishop 1941:253). Nocturnal, forages for food among rocks and vegetation in or along stream beds on rainy summer nights. Larvae are generalist feeders until metamorphosis, when they take larger food items (Bruce 1980).

Comments. Formerly named the purple salamander.

Selected references. Bishop 1941; Brandon 1967; Bruce 1972, 1980.

Northern two-lined salamander

Eurycea b. bislineata
Caudata
Plethodontidae

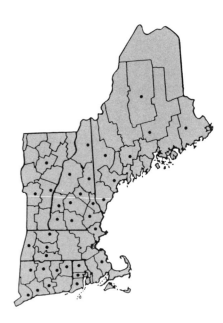

Range. Gaspé Peninsula, Quebec, and e. Ontario southwest through Ohio to e. Illinois, south to extreme n.e. Mississippi to Virginia.

Relative abundance. Common to abundant.

Habitat. Flood-plain bottoms to moist forest floors at high elevations to 6,000 ft (1,829 m) (Behler and King 1979:321). Along brooks and streams, boggy areas near springs or seeps. Found under objects at water's edge in moist soil or in coarse sand and gravel at stream bottoms or edges, leaf litter and crayfish burrows (Ashton and Ashton 1978). In wet woodlands or pastures. During wet or humid weather it will wander into moist woods over 100 m from water courses.

It hibernates under water, or remains active in feeding aggregations in springs and cold flowing streams in New York (Stewart 1956a). Also found in unfrozen soil of stream banks (Ashton and Ashton 1978).

Special habitat requirements. Streams with high pH for breeding.

Age/size at sexual maturity. The majority mature during the second fall after metamorphosis (Stewart 1956a).

Breeding period and egg deposition. Breeds in streams in autumn and early spring. Eggs deposited from May to early June, Massachusetts (Johnson and Goldberg 1975).

No. eggs/mass. 12 to 36 eggs, average of 18 eggs in Massachusetts (Wilder 1924). Eggs deposited in clusters attached to bottoms of stones or logs in running water. Several females may use the same stone as a nest site, one female remains with eggs until hatching.

Eggs hatch. 1 to 2 months after eggs laid.

Larval period. 2 or 3 years, aquatic (Wilder 1924).

Home range/movement. Average area less than 14 m² for 20 monitored individuals along a stream in Ohio (Ashton and Ashton 1978). Territories were aggressively defended in an artificial environment (Grant 1955).

Food habits/preferences. Insects, particularly beetles, beetle larvae, mayflies, stonefly nymphs, and dipterans; also spiders, mites, millipedes, sowbugs, and earthworms (Hamilton 1932). Most prey are of terrestrial origin (Burton 1976).

Comments. Will travel in the open during wet or rainy nights, rarely during wet days. Adults are extremely agile and when disturbed often escape through a series of rapid jumps.

Selected references. Bishop 1941; Bleakney 1958; Mittleman 1966.

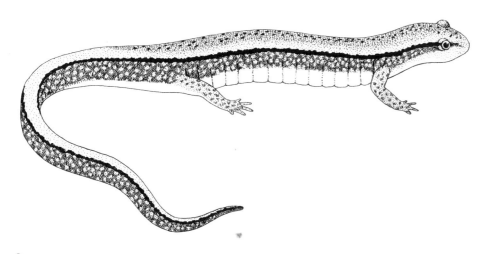

Toads
and Frogs

(order Anura)

Nine families of frogs and toads occur in North America, and include eighty-one species north of Mexico. In New England, four families occur: two of toads, the Pelobatidae and Bufonidae; and two of frogs, the Hylidae and Ranidae. They include eleven species. The most boreal, the mink frog (*Rana septentrionalis*), has the southern limit of its range within the region. Northeastern range limits for the Fowler's toad *(Bufo woodhousii fowleri)* and eastern spadefoot *(Scaphiopus h. holbrookii)* are in New England.

Anurans, the frogs and toads, are extremely vocal during breeding season. The vocalization of males helps to attract females to lakes, ponds, or even rain pools. All species lay eggs in fresh water. Some adults are arboreal, some are aquatic, while others are terrestrial. Eggs develop into tadpoles (these larvae are called locally pollywogs in some parts of New England). Metamorphosis of the tadpole may be rapid, as in the spadefoot, where development from egg to juvenile may be completed in two weeks, or delayed, as in the bullfrog *(Rana catesbeiana)*, in which case tadpoles may not transform until the following year.

The Pelobatidae, or spadefoot toad family, contains only one North American genus, *Scaphiopus,* with five species. New England has a single species, the eastern spadefoot. The common name comes from the horny, sharp-edged tubercle or ''spade'' on the inner surface of the hind foot. This species is fossorial and digs burrows in loose soil. (Frogs and, to a lesser extent, toads easily become dessicated; those that are adapted to dry areas burrow into the soil during the heat of the day or hide under rocks or logs.) Spade-foots are further differentiated in the field from true toads by the teeth along the upper jaw, vertical pupils, and smoother skin. They often breed in temporary rain pools that may disappear within a few weeks (Behler and King 1979:362).

The true toad family, the Bufonidae, contains one North American genus, *Bufo;* two species occur in New England, the American *(B. a. americanus)* and Fowler's. Toads have rough, warty skin (toxic skin secretions irritate mucous membranes of some predators), horizontal pupils, and they lack teeth on the upper jaw.

The tree frog family (Hylidae) contains seven North American genera, one of which is in New England, containing two species. Treefrogs are small, with slender legs and horizontal pupils. All the New England species typically walk and climb, aided by adhesive discs on their toes. Males call from perches over or near the water.

True frogs (Ranidae) are represented by a single genus in North America: *Rana.* New England contains six species. Ranids have a bony breastbone and horizontal pupils; North American species are large, slim-waisted, and long-toed, and they have extensive webbing on the hind feet (Behler and King 1979:367).

Eastern spadefoot

Scaphiopus h. holbrookii
Anura
Pelobatidae

Range. Southeastern Massachusetts extending to New York and s.e. Missouri, south to e. Louisiana and Florida. Not found in the higher elevations of the Appalachians or the Everglades of Florida.

Relative abundance. Rare; more common south into New Jersey, Maryland, and Delaware.

Habitat. Dry sandy or loose soils in sparse shrub growth or open forest areas. Terrestrial and subterranean, it only enters water to breed, usually in temporary rain pools. Prefers forest areas with leaf litter (Pearson 1955). In oak-hickory savanna in Oklahoma, in farmland areas in the Connecticut River Valley, Massachusetts, and pitch-pine–scrub oak dunes in New York (Stewart and Rossi 1981). Colonies occur along flood plains of major rivers. Emerge in spring from hibernation when soil moisture is sufficient.

Special habitat requirements. Sandy soils, temporary pools for breeding.

Age/size at sexual maturity. During second year after metamorphosis, males at 15 months, females at 19 months (Pearson 1955).

Breeding period and egg deposition. Usually April or May, extending into August; breeding is initiated by a heavy rainfall (Gosner and Black 1955). Breeds in congregations of many individuals if population is high. Usually a one-night phenomenon.

No. eggs/mass. 1,000 to 2,500 eggs in masses of 6 to 110 in irregular bands in or around vegetation in temporary pools. Eggs are very adhesive.

Eggs hatch. 5 to 15 days (Oliver 1955:236).

Tadpoles. Late broods transform in 16 to 20 days (Gosner and Black 1955), 48 to 63 days for early broods (Driver 1936).

Home range/movement. Overall mean home range of marked individuals was about 108 ft² (10 m²) in n. Florida, but 90% had an average home range of about 67 ft² (6.2 m²). Occupy one or several underground burrows within home range (Pearson 1955). Maximum dispersal distances of 32 ft (9.8 m); individuals were recaptured in the same home ranges after 5 years (Pearson 1957).

Food habits/preferences. Flies, spiders, crickets, caterpillars, true bugs, other ground-dwelling arthropods, earthworms, and snails. Moths are eaten when they can be caught (Bragg 1965:36). Tadpoles are planktonic feeders for the first few days (Richmond 1947), later becoming carnivorous and sometimes even cannibalistic.

Comments. Nocturnal: peaks of activity occur just after sundown and before sunrise. Fossorial: individuals have remained in burrows an average of 9.5 days at a time, emerging to feed (Pearson 1955). Can remain

underground for weeks or months during dry periods, to depths of 3 to 7 ft (1 to 2 m) (Ball 1933 in Babbitt 1937:20). As evidence of the spadefoot's secretive and nocturnal habits, only 16 sightings were reported from 1811 to 1936 in the northeastern part of its range (Ball 1936, cited in Bragg 1965:51).

Selected references. Ball 1936; Pearson 1955; Bragg 1965; Wasserman 1968.

Eastern American toad

Bufo a. americanus
Anura
Bufonidae

Range. Nova Scotia and the Gaspé Peninsula west through central Ontario to Lake Winnipeg, south throughout New England to e. Kansas, central Indiana, central Alabama, and central North Carolina.
Relative abundance. Common.
Habitat. Found in almost any habitat: gardens, woods, yards with cover, damp soil, and a food supply. Sea level to mountain elevations. Usually in moist upland woods.
Special habitat requirements. Needs shallow water for breeding. Hibernates in underground burrows to 12 in (30.4 cm) deep (Oliver 1955:122) from October to late March or April.
Age/size at sexual maturity. 3 to 4 years (Dickerson 1969:72); 2 to 3 years (Hamilton 1934).

Breeding period and egg deposition. Early April to July, peak in late April in the Northeast. Travels to breeding ponds at night in large numbers (Maynard 1934).
No. eggs/mass. 4,000 to 12,000 eggs (Dickerson 1969:67). Laid in long curling strings amidst aquatic vegetation.
Eggs hatch. About 3 to 12 (average 4) days.
Tadpoles. 5 to 10 weeks.
Home range/movement. Exhibits homing behavior by returning to breeding sites; 264 individuals used the same site annually in Ontario (Oldham 1966).
Food habits/preferences. Terrestrial arthropods, including insects, sowbugs, spiders, centipedes, and millipedes. Slugs and earthworms are other invertebrate foods. Some vegetable matter is taken accidentally. Food species determined by availability (Hamilton 1954). Feeds from twilight through the evening hours.
Comments. Most active during evening hours. May bask (M. Stewart,

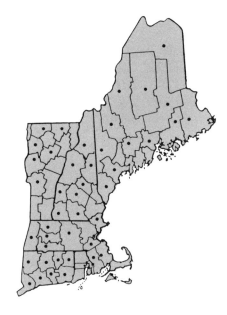

L. White, pers. observ.), but will seek cover during the heat of the day. Calls and breeds during the day at the peak of breeding season (T. Tyning, pers. commun.).
Selected references. Wright and Wright 1949; Hamilton 1954.

Fowler's toad

Bufo woodhousii fowleri
Anura
Bufonidae

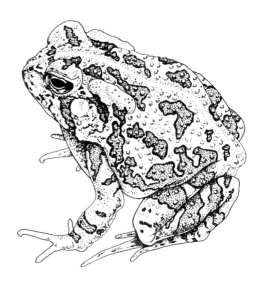

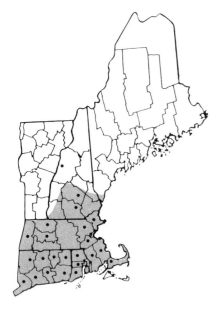

Range. Southern New England west to central Pennsylvania, the n. shore of Lake Erie and e. shore of Lake Michigan south to Missouri, e. Oklahoma, Texas, central Georgia, and South Carolina.

Relative abundance. Locally common.

Habitat. Prefers areas with sandy soil—shorelines, river valleys, beaches, and roadside areas. Usually found in lowland areas, but frequently in pine and oak forests, gardens, lawns, and fields; also found in small marshy ponds. Hibernates in burrows in well-drained sandy soils to 3 ft (0.9 m) deep from early fall to late spring (May in Connecticut).

Special habitat requirements. Sandy soils, shallow water for breeding.

Age/size at sexual maturity. Probably breeds during third year (Stille 1952).

Breeding period and egg deposition. Late April to May extending to mid-August (2 to 4 weeks later than *B. a. americanus*). Shallow water of pools, lake margins, ditches, etc., necessary for breeding.

No. eggs/mass. Up to 8,000 eggs laid in long strings in aquatic vegetation (Wright and Wright 1949:212).

Eggs hatch. About 1 week.

Tadpoles. 40 to 60 days, usually transform midsummer.

Home range/movement. Average distances between captures ranged from 22 to 32 m during a 3-year period on a golf course in Connecticut (Clarke 1974). Night movements of 200 to 700 ft (61 to 213 m) or more to reach water's edge (Lake Michigan). Toads usually found within 100 ft (30.5 m) of previous capture point (Stille 1952).

Food habits/preferences. Chiefly ground-dwelling insects, particularly ants and beetles; also consumes earthworms, spiders, snails, and slugs.

Comments. During evening hours may move to edge of water to replenish body moisture (Stille 1952). May be active during the day, but typically crepuscular (Minton 1972:95). Activity periods vary with populations, mostly nocturnal in Connecticut (Clarke 1974).

Selected references. Wright and Wright 1949; Logier 1952; Clarke 1974.

Northern spring peeper

Hyla c. crucifer
Anura
Hylidae

Range. Nova Scotia, the Gaspé Peninsula and Quebec to the s. tip of Hudson Bay through Ontario to Lake Winnipeg, south throughout New England to e. Texas and throughout the e. United States except Florida and s. Georgia.

Relative abundance. Common to abundant.

Habitat. Marshy or wet woods, second growth woodlots, sphagnum bogs, nonwooded lowlands, near ponds and swamps. Found on the ground or burrowed into the soil. Breeds in permanent or temporary water, usually woodland ponds with aquatic debris. Found in cool moist woods after breeding (M. Stewart, pers. observ.). Hibernates on land during late November to January or early spring, under moss and leaves.

Special habitat requirements. Pools for breeding.

Age/size at sexual maturity. Early in second year at about 20 mm (Delzell 1958).

Breeding period and egg deposition. Early March to June (in the North). *No. eggs/mass.* 800 to 1,000 eggs (Wright 1914:16). Laid singly near the bottom of shallow weedy ponds, attached to submerged plants (Oliver 1955:236).

Eggs hatch. 6 to 12 days.

Tadpoles. 90 to 100 days (Wright 1914:42). Usually transform during July (Wright and Wright 1949:314).

Home range/movement. In s.e. Michigan, home range diameters ranged from 4 to 18 ft (1.2 to 5.5 m), established around forest debris and vegetation; average daily travel was 20 to 130 ft (6.1 to 39.6 m) as reported by Delzell (1958).

Food habits/preferences. Small nonaquatic insects: preferably ants, flying bugs, beetles, flies, springtails, and spiders; also mites, ticks, and small snails. Foods taken probably reflect availability and size, rather than preference (Oplinger 1967).

Comments. Young frogs terrestrial in first year (Delzell 1958). May move long distances from breeding areas in summer and fall, single calls heard from woods, shrubby openings, far from water (M. Stewart, pers. observ.).

Selected references. Wright and Wright 1949; Logier 1952; Delzell 1958.

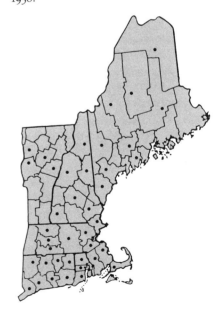

Gray treefrog

Hyla versicolor
Anura
Hylidae

Range. Eastern United States and
s.e. Canada from s. Maine to Mani-
toba and south through central
Texas and the Gulf States to central
Florida.
Relative abundance. Common.
Habitat. Forested regions with small

trees, shrubs, and bushes near or in
shallow water. Often found on moss
or lichen on bark of old trees. Breeds
in temporary pools or permanent
water, swamps, bogs, ponds,
weedy lakes, and roadside ditches,
but breeding sites are extremely variable. Commonly inhabits moist
areas in hollow trees, under loose
bark, or in rotted logs during summer months (Smith 1961:93). Hibernates under tree roots, under leaves
(Babbitt 1937).
Special habitat requirements. Aquatic
sites for breeding.
Age/size at sexual maturity. Breeds at
3 years (Palmer 1949:455).
Breeding period and egg deposition.
Early May to July, Connecticut (Babbitt 1937). May to August (Martof et
al. 1980:116). Season varies with latitude (Smith 1961:93). Peak in early
May, Ithaca, New York (Wright
1914:44). Generally 20 to 35 days
elapse between first appearance of
adults and first eggs (Wright
1914:47). Loosely attached to vegetation on the surface of shallow

water (Martof et al. 1980:116).
No. eggs/mass. Total of 1,800 to 2,000
eggs (Wright 1914:49). Packets of
10 to 40 eggs (Martof et al. 1980:116);
4 to 25 eggs (Smith 1961:93).
Eggs hatch. 4 to 5 days (Babbitt 1937).
Tadpoles. 50 to 60 days, shorter periods in warmer areas. Transform late
in June to September.
Home range/movement. Unreported.
Food habits/preferences. Small insects,
spiders, plant lice, mites, snails.
Forages in vegetation and on the
ground (Martof et al. 1980:116).
Comments. Most active during evening hours when vocal both during
and out of breeding season. Rarely
found outside of breeding period.
Able to change color from gray to
green. Young are emerald green.
Single calls heard occasionally in
summer during humid days, often
before a storm. *H. versicolor* is a tetra-
ploid species with 48 chromosomes
(Martof et al. 1980:115).
Selected references. Wright and
Wright 1949; Logier 1952; Martof et
al. 1980.

Bullfrog

Rana catesbeiana
Anura
Ranidae

Range. Nova Scotia west to Wisconsin, south through the Great Plains to e. Colorado, Texas, and n.e. Mexico; throughout the e. United States except s. Florida and parts of n. Maine. Introduced in California and British Columbia.

Relative abundance. Common.

Habitat. Near shorelines of large bodies of water with emergent vegetation, lakes, river oxbows. Highly aquatic. Tends to remain in same pools for the summer months if water level is stable (Raney 1940). Will occupy floating logs far from shore. Breeds close to shorelines in areas sheltered by shrubs (Raney 1940). Hibernates in mud and leaves under water about mid-October,

emerges late February to March, May in New York (Wright 1914:78).

Special habitat requirements. Deep permanent water and emergent vegetation.

Age/size at sexual maturity. In fourth or fifth year.

Breeding period and egg deposition. Late May to July (in the North), peak in July.

No. eggs/mass. 12,000 to 20,000 eggs (Wright 1914:82). Eggs laid in floating films of jelly in water of lakes, quiet streams, and ponds.

Eggs hatch. 5 to 20 days (Oliver 1955:237). Often 4 days or less (Wright 1914:83).

Tadpoles. For 2 or 3 winters.

Home range/movement. Average distance traveled in summer, 200 to 300 ft (61 to 91 m) in a woodland lake and pond in New York (Raney 1940; Ingram and Raney 1943). Evening movement of 200 to 700 ft (61 to 213 m) to water in Michigan (Stille 1952).

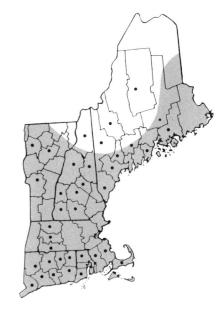

Home range of 131 bullfrogs in an Ontario pond had an average mean activity radius of 8.6 ft (2.6 m) with minimum and maximum movements of 2.0 ft (0.6 m) and 37.1 ft (11.3 m) respectively (Currie and Bellis 1969). Males defend territories during breeding season. In a Michigan study (Emlen 1968), the average distance between males within a chorus was 17.8 ft (5.4 m), implying an average minimum territorial radius of approximately 9 ft (2.7 m).

Food habits/preferences. Any available small animals; fish, other frogs, salamanders, newts, young turtles, snakes, small birds, mice, crayfish, insects, snails, and spiders. Also cannibalistic. Feeds among the water weeds; an indiscriminate and aggressive predator.

Comments. The bullfrog has become rare in many areas, presumably due to toxic effects of DDT and other pollutants (M. Stewart, pers. commun.). The threat of overharvest has led to regulation of the bullfrog as a game animal in some states.

Selected references. Wright and Wright 1949; Logier 1952.

Green frog
Rana clamitans melanota
Anura
Ranidae

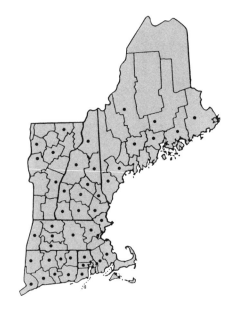

Range. Nova Scotia through Quebec
and s. Ontario to central Minnesota,
south to e. Oklahoma and east to n.
Georgia and South Carolina. Absent
from central Illinois.
Relative abundance. Common.
Habitat. Margins of shallow permanent or semipermanent fresh water,
shores and banks of lakes and
ponds, creeks, woodland streams,
limestone quarry pools, springs,
vernal pools, moist woodlands near
water. Seldom more than a few
meters from the water. Young often
found in semipermanent water.
Hibernates underground or underwater from October until March,
usually within its home range
(Martof 1953b). May be active on
warm winter days.
Special habitat requirements. Riparian
areas.
Age/size at sexual maturity. Males sexually active the season following
metamorphosis when 60 to 65 mm

long; females mature during the second or third year when 65 to 75 mm
long (Martof 1956). Some females
reached maturity at 90 mm at Cranberry Lake, New York (M. Stewart,
pers. commun.). Some may not
breed until the second year after
transformation (Wells 1977).
Breeding period and egg deposition.
April to August, peak in mid-May,
varies with locality. The same female may lay two clutches (Wells

1976). Emerges from hibernation in
early spring but does not breed until
mid-May in Connecticut (Babbitt
1937).
No. eggs/mass. 3,500 to 4,000 eggs
(Wright 1914:16); 5,000 (Pope 1944).
Eggs deposited in floating masses of
jelly attached to underwater twigs
and stems in permanent water.
Eggs hatch. 3 to 6 days (Babbitt 1937).
Tadpoles. 1 to 2 years. Less than 1
year in southern parts of range. May
transform in same season eggs are
laid (Martof 1956).
Home range/movement. Varied from
20 m² to 200 m² with an average of
61 m² in s. Michigan near a stream
and lake; daily movements were less
than 10 m for 80% of the 824 individuals recaptured (Martof 1953b).
During breeding season, males
maintained a 2 to 3 m distance between each other (Martof 1953a).
Territory size dependent upon cover
density, 1 to 1.5 m beween males in
areas of dense cover. Territories
with diameters of 4 to 6 m defended
in open areas in New York (Wells
1977).
Food habits/preferences. Terrestrial
feeders among shoreline vegetation.
Insects and their larvae, worms,
small fish, crayfish and other crustaceans, newts, spiders, small frogs,
and mollusks are taken. Beetles,
flies, grasshoppers, and caterpillars
constituted over 60% of food items
(Hamilton 1948). Terrestrial beetles
are the most important food item
(Stewart and Sandison 1972). Tadpoles are herbivorous.
Comments. Green frogs are found in
or at the edge of water during day-
light hours; evening hours spent
along the banks feeding or in water
defending territories (Wells 1977).
Selected references. Wright and
Wright 1949; Logier 1952; Martof
1953b, 1956.

Mink frog

Rana septentrionalis
Anura
Ranidae

Range. Nova Scotia, n. New England and New York west to n. Wisconsin and Minnesota, north through Ontario to St. James Bay and to n. Quebec and Labrador.
Relative abundance. Only in extreme northern areas, locally common to rare.
Habitat. Edges of northern lakes and ponds, cold springs, inlets where cold streams enter ponds and stream edges. Prefers open water with abundant lily pads. Sometimes found in northern bogs.
Special habitat requirements. Breeds and hibernates only in permanent waters. Prefers lily pads in open water for basking and foraging (M. Stewart, pers. commun.).
Age/size at sexual maturity. Males 1 year after metamorphosis, females 1 to 2 years after metamorphosis (Hedeen 1972).
Breeding period and egg deposition. June to early August (Hedeen 1972),

peak in July (Wright and Wright 1949:535).
No. eggs/mass. One individual laid 509 eggs (Hedeen 1972). Eggs laid in globular jellylike masses attached to underwater vegetation such as spatterdock *(Nuphar),* then drop to bottom where they develop (M. Stewart, pers. commun.).
Eggs hatch. Unreported.
Tadpoles. For 1 to 2 years. Transform during summer months.

Home range/movement. Unreported.
Food habits/preferences. Adults feed from lily pads on animal matter, including adult insects and larvae, particularly aphids and chrysomelids (Kramek 1972, 1976); also minnows, millipedes, leeches, snails, spiders; plant material taken inadvertently. Most prey taken from the water surface—usually opportunistic feeders but can be selective (Kramek 1972). Diet is a reflection of prey species availability. Tadpoles feed primarily on algae (Hedeen 1970).
Comments. Very similar to *R. clamitans melanota* in appearance and habits. Adults produce a musky scent, especially when handled roughly (Conant 1975:342). Competition from green frogs and bullfrogs may be an important factor in habitat selection in the Northeast (M. Stewart, pers. commun.). In ponds treated with rotenone in the Adirondacks, the anuran community of green, mink, and bullfrogs probably requires 10 to 15 years to recover to pretreatment levels (Stewart 1975).
Selected references. Logier 1952; Marshall and Buell 1955; Hedeen 1977.

Wood frog

Rana sylvatica
Anura
Ranidae

Range. Atlantic provinces and n. Quebec to Alaska (northern limit is along treeline) south into North Dakota, the Great Lakes States, to the Appalachians in Tennessee and extreme n. Georgia. Throughout the Northeast.

Relative abundance. Common in suitable habitat.

Habitat. Mesic woods, often far from water during the summer months as woodland ponds dry up; xeric woods with moist microhabitats (M. Klemens, pers. commun.). Prefers wooded areas with small ponds for breeding (Heatwole 1961). Found in boreal conifer forests, swamps, and upland hardwood forests to elevations of 3,800 ft (1,158 m) (Trapido and Clausen 1938). Found in bogs and trap rock slopes in Connecticut (M. Klemens, pers. commun.). Hibernates under moist forest floor debris or flooded meadows (M. Klemens, pers. commun.) from October to late March. Embryos and larvae showed limited tolerance to water with a high humic content in a Minnesota peat bog (Karns 1980).

Special habitat requirements. Terrestrial, it prefers temporary woodland pools, back waters of slow-moving streams.

Age/size at sexual maturity. Males at 2 years, females at 3 years (Bellis 1961).

Breeding period and egg deposition. March to July at temperatures of about 10 C (Smith 1956:113). Often breeds before ice is off the water (Martof 1970:86.2). Egg laying usually completed within 4 to 6 days (Herreid and Kinney 1967).

No. eggs/mass. 2,000 to 3,000 eggs (Wright 1914:16); 1,019 average in Massachusetts (Possardt 1974). Eggs attached to submerged twigs or free on the bottom in globular masses.

Eggs hatch. 10 to 30 days (Oliver 1955:236), temperature dependent.

Tadpoles. 6 to 15 weeks (Minton 1972:132). May overwinter in n. Canada.

Home range/movement. Average home range size for 453 individuals in a Minnesota peat bog was 77.2 yd² (64.5 m²), range 3.5 to 440.5 yd² (2.9 to 368.3 m²). Distance between captures averaged 12.3 yd (11.2 m) and ranged from 0 to 78 yd (0 to 71.3 m) as reported by Bellis (1965).

Food habits/preferences. Insects; particularly beetles, flies, and hyme-

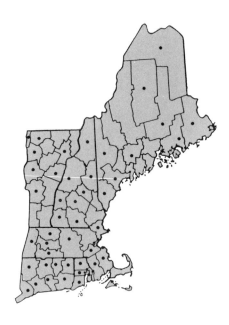

nopterans (Moore and Strickland 1955); also spiders, snails, slugs, and annelids.

Comments. Breeds before all other ranids in the Northeast. Adults have been observed migrating across surface ice toward chorusing wood frogs (T. Andrews, pers. observ.). Brush piles, grassy hummocks, and other terrestrial objects used as cover rather than utilizing aquatic escape (Marshall and Buell 1955).

Selected references. Wright and Wright 1949; Heatwole 1961; Martof 1970.

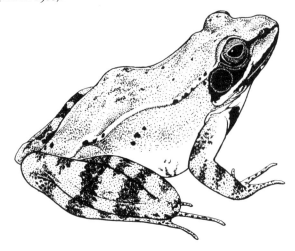

Northern leopard frog

Rana pipiens
Anura
Ranidae

Range. Nova Scotia, s. Labrador to s.e. British Columbia, south to e. parts of Oregon, Washington, and California, to n. Arizona and New Mexico, and east to Ohio, n. New York, and New England.

Relative abundance. Locally common; spotty distributions in southern part of range, very uncommon in some parts of formerly occupied range.

Habitat. Commonly found in wet open meadows and fields and wet woods during summer months. River flood plains, Connecticut (M. Klemens, pers. commun.). Breeds in ponds, marshes, slow shallow streams, weedy lake inlets. Usually hibernates from October or November to March, hibernates under water in or on muddy bottoms or in caves (Rand 1950). Sometimes emerges in early February (Smith 1956:110) and during warm days in winter (Zenisek 1964).

Special habitat requirements. Wet meadows.

Age/size at sexual maturity. At 3 years of age in Michigan (Force 1933).

Breeding period and egg deposition. March to May, congregates to breed (Wright and Wright 1949:482).

No. eggs/mass. 4,000 to 6,500 eggs laid in masses in shallow water, sometimes attached to twigs.

Eggs hatch. 13 to 20 days (Wright 1914:58).

Tadpoles. 9 to 12 weeks, transform July and August. Overwinter as tadpoles in Nova Scotia (Bleakney 1952).

Home range/movement. Daily travel within home range reported to be usually less than 5 to 10 m in wet pasture and marsh (Dole 1965).

Average nightly movement during rainy periods was 36 m in Michigan (Dole 1968). Occasional long-range movement, often exceeding 100 m during rainy nights (Dole 1965).

Food habits/preferences. Insects, particularly beetles, lepidopteran larvae, wasps, bugs, crickets, grasshoppers, and ants; also takes sowbugs, spiders, small crayfish, snails, and myriopods. Almost 99% of food items were insects and spiders (Drake 1914). Occasional records of having taken small birds and snakes. Food species taken correlates with peaks in insect prey abundance (Linzey 1967).

Comments. During dry summer days frogs may sit in "forms," small clearings made in wet soil within their home range (Dole 1965). Some populations in New England may have

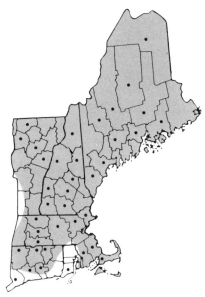

been introduced (T. Tyning, pers. commun.).

Selected references. Logier 1952; Dole 1968.

Pickerel frog
Rana palustris
Anura
Ranidae

Range. Nova Scotia and the Gaspé Peninsula through s.e. Ontario to Wisconsin south to e. Texas and east to South Carolina. Absent from central Illinois, n.w. Ohio, and parts of the South.

Relative abundance. Locally common.

Habitat. Colder waters of lakes, ponds, clear streams, springs, sphagnum bogs, limestone quarry pools. In Massachusetts, fairly ubiquitous along streams and shores of permanent ponds and lakes (T. Andrews, pers. commun.). In summer, found in pastures, fields, or woodlands, often at a distance from water. Prefers water with thick vegetation at edges for cover. Hibernates in mud at bottom of ponds or in ravines under stones from October to March. Some individuals found wintering in caves in Indiana (Rand 1950).

Special habitat requirements. Shallow, clear water of bogs and woodland

ponds for breeding.

Age/size at sexual maturity. Breeds at 2 to 3 years (Palmer 1949:457).

Breeding period and egg deposition. March to May.

No. eggs/mass. 2,000 to 3,000 eggs (Wright 1914:67). Eggs laid in firm globular masses attached to submerged plants and branches.

Eggs hatch. 11 to 21 days (Wright 1914:67).

Tadpoles. 80 to 100 days. Transform July to September. Some tadpoles overwinter, transforming the following spring.

Home range/movement. Unreported.

Food habits/preferences. In adults, 95% of food items were terrestrial arthropods (Smith 1956:108). Snails, small crayfish, aquatic amphipods, and isopods are also eaten.

Comments. Diurnal; may be crepuscular during hot weather. Sensitive to pollution and changes in water quality. Skin secretions may be toxic

to other amphibians confined with pickerel frogs.

Selected references. Wright and Wright 1949; Smith 1956; Schaaf and Smith 1971.

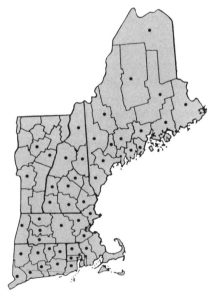

Turtles
(order Testudines)

Seven families of turtles occur in the United States and Canada; New England contains four families: the Chelydridae, Kinosternidae, Emydidae, and Trionychidae. Of the thirteen species and subspecies of turtles (excluding sea turtles) in New England, one has been introduced: the red-eared slider *(Pseudemys scripta elegans)*, into Massachusetts and Connecticut. Excluding Canada, New England is the northeastern range limit of the bog *(Clemmys muhlenbergii)*, eastern box *(Terrapene c. carolina)*, stinkpot *(Sternotherus odoratus)*, eastern spiny softshell *(Trionyx s. spiniferus)*, and Blanding's *(Emydoidea blandingii)* turtles. One subspecies, the Plymouth redbelly turtle *(Pseudemys rubriventris bangsi)*, is restricted to Massachusetts.

The snapping turtle family (Chelydridae) is represented by a single species in New England, the common snapping turtle *(Chelydra s. serpentina)*. The family consists of two New World genera, each represented by a single species in the United States. Snapping turtles have large heads, hooked jaws, long tails, and small cross-shaped plastrons. The carapaces have twelve marginal scutes along each side (Behler and King 1979:435).

The musk and mud turtles (Kinosternidae) are restricted to the Americas. In New England, there is one representative of the family: the stinkpot *(Sternotherus odoratus)*. Musk turtles have smooth, oval carapaces with eleven marginal scutes on each side; the rear margin of the carapace is not serrated, and the plastron is single- or double-hinged with ten or eleven scutes. The plastron of the stinkpot has a single inconspicuous hinge. All musk turtles have two pairs of musk glands beneath the carapace border (Behler and King 1979:448).

The pond, marsh, and box turtle family (Emydidae) is well represented in the eastern United States, and ten of the thirteen inland turtles of New England are members of this family. Emydids are small to midsized turtles with twelve marginal carapace scutes along each side and six pairs of scutes on the plastron. The elongated hind feet have some webbing. Basking is a common behavioral trait (Behler and King 1979:446).

A single member of the softshell turtle family, or Trionychidae, occurs in New England, and only along the eastern shore of Lake Champlain. The flattened carapace of the eastern spiny softshell is soft and leathery and nearly circular. The feet are fully webbed and have three claws. The snout is tube shaped, and is used as a breathing snorkle while, except for the snout, the turtle swims submerged (Behler and King 1979:483).

Common snapping turtle

Chelydra s. serpentina
Testudines
Chelydridae

Range. Across the e. United States to the Rocky Mountains, s. Canada to the Gulf of Mexico and into Central America.

Relative abundance. Common.

Habitat. Any permanent and many semipermanent bodies of fresh or brackish water; occasionally in temporary water. Marshes, swamps, bogs, pools, lakes, streams, rivers, frequently in areas with soft muddy banks or bottoms. Formerly thought to prefer permanent water. A bottom dweller and almost entirely aquatic, it will travel overland. Hibernates from October to March or April in mud or debris in lake bottoms, banks, and muskrat holes, but has been seen walking on and under the ice (Carr 1952:64). Little known about winter activity.

Special habitat requirements. Aquatic habitat.

Age/size at sexual maturity. Carapace length of 10 in (25.4 cm) as reported by Hammer (1969).

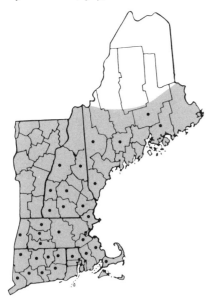

Breeding period. Late April to November, sperm may remain viable in females for several years.

Egg deposition. Mid-June. Nests made in soil of banks or in muskrat houses. Also on lawns, driveways, fields, sometimes far from water.

Clutch size. 11 to 83 eggs; females may lay two clutches per year in southern portions of range. Typically 20 to 30 eggs per clutch (Cahn 1937 cited in Conant 1938:128).

Incubation period. 55 to 125 days (Hammer 1969), typically 80 to 91 days, but dependent upon environmental conditions.

Eggs hatch. Late August to early October, may overwinter in nest until spring in northern portions of range. Nests often destroyed by mammalian predators.

Home range/movement. In a New York marsh, movement of 100 m was the average for 85 individuals; home ranges of 3 to 9 ha (Kiviat 1980). Average distance traveled by 107 individuals was 0.69 mi (1.1 km), with most movement within the same marsh in South Dakota (Hammer 1969). Established range in Pennsylvania 4.5 ac (1.8 ha), re-ported by Ernst (1968b). Quite migratory. Females exhibit strong nesting site fidelity and will travel more than 0.5 km overland through forest and uneven terrain between water bodies in Ontario. Maximum round-trip distance of 16 km between home range and nesting site (Obbard and Brooks 1980).

Food habits/preferences. Omnivorous feeders; animal matter comprising 54% of prey items including fish (40%), crayfish, aquatic invertebrates, reptiles, birds, mammals; plant material 37% (Alexander 1943). Primary fish species in diet included suckers, bullheads, sunfish, and perch in Connecticut (Alexander 1943). May occasionally take young waterfowl; not destructive to natural populations of fish or waterfowl. Scavenges for any food readily available.

Comments. High levels of persisting organochlorine contaminants found in the tissues of Hudson River specimens (Stone et al. 1980).

Selected references. Babcock 1919; Hammer 1969; Kiviat 1980.

Stinkpot

Sternotherus odoratus
Testudines
Kinosternidae

Range. Atlantic coast, s. Ontario, west to the Mississippi River, south to central Texas, s. Florida. Absent from n. New England.

Relative abundance. Locally common.

Habitat. Permanent bodies of water: still, shallow, clear lakes, ponds, and rivers, muddy bottoms preferred. Frequently found in reservoirs (M. Klemens, pers. commun.). Refrains from using temporary water sources. Formerly thought to refrain from using water with fluctuating levels. Not in streams at higher elevations in the East. Large populations found in areas with abundant aquatic vegetation (Pope 1939:39). Scattered records for occurrence in marshes, swamps, bogs, sloughs (Pope 1939:39). Usually gregarious when hibernating in bottom mud, debris, beneath rocks in river bottoms, or in river banks when the temperature falls below 10 C (Cagle 1942).

Special habitat requirements. Permanent water bodies. Exclusively aquatic except when laying eggs.

Age/size at sexual maturity. Stinkpots in the northern portion of the range mature more slowly than individuals in the southern regions. Males at 3 or 4 years, females at 2 to 7 years (Tinkle 1961), or perhaps at 9 to 11 years (Risely 1932).

Breeding period. April to October, peaks in April to May and September to October.

Egg deposition. May to August, peak in June. Eggs laid in muck, rotted logs, stumps, sandy soil, grass, or on the ground at lake margins.

Clutch size. 1 to 9 eggs (highest numbers in North), typically 3 to 6.

Incubation period. 60 to 90 days (Barbour 1971:162), 35 to 40 days (Edgren 1960).

Eggs hatch. September to October (in North). Gregarious nesting habits, often malodorous.

Home range/movement. Overland movements probably seasonal or forced (Ernst and Barbour 1972:40). Average home ranges of 0.6 ac (0.02 ha) for males and 0.12 ac (0.05 ha) for females in Oklahoma. Overland movements ranged from 166 to 227 ft (35.4 to 69.2 m) for males, and 113 to 146 ft (34.4 to 44.5 m) for females (Mahmoud 1969). Exhibited homing behavior in Michigan—13 of 28 released individuals traveled up to 700 ft (213 m) to initial capture points (Williams 1952).

Food habits/preferences. Principally carnivorous, feeds along the bottom for snails, clams, aquatic insects and their larvae, particularly dragonfly nymphs and caddisfly larvae (Lagler 1943); minnows, worms, tadpoles, and fish eggs (Babcock 1919:36). Plants and algae are often taken while scavenging. Carrion comprised 40 % of the diet by volume for 73 individuals in Michigan (Lagler 1943).

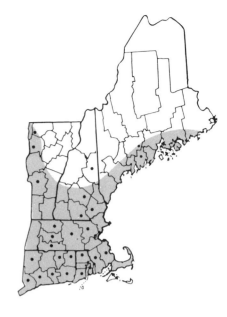

Comments. Also called the musk turtle. Often basks well out of water on horizontal limbs of slanting trees along the water's edge and on logs and rocks. Highly aquatic; activity periods in morning and evening in Oklahoma (Mahmoud 1968). Individuals frequently covered with algae growth.

Selected references. Mahmoud 1969; Ernst and Barbour 1972.

Spotted turtle

Clemmys guttata
Testudines
Emydidae

Range. Southern Maine to s. Quebec west to Lake Michigan, n. half of Ohio to e. portion of Virginia south to n. Florida.

Relative abundance. Uncommon to rare.

Habitat. Unpolluted, small shallow bodies of water such as woodland streams, wet meadows, bog holes, small ponds, marshes, swamps, roadside ditches, and brackish tidal creeks. In Rhode Island found in salt marshes and small bogs or ponds with adjacent dry upland oak-pine forest (C. Raithel, pers. commun.). Prefers areas with aquatic vegetation. Hides in mud and detritus at bottom. Wanders over land. Basks along water's edge on brush piles in water (T. Graham, pers. commun.) and on logs or vegetation clumps. Often found in cranberry bogs. Hibernates in muddy bottoms during the coldest winter months. May aestivate during hottest periods of summer (T. Tyning, pers. commun.).

Special habitat requirements. Unpolluted shallow water.

Age/size at sexual maturity. Males about 83.4 mm plastron length, females about 80.8 mm plastron length in Pennsylvania (Ernst and Barbour 1972:73).

Breeding period. March to May, peak usually in June.

Egg deposition. June to July. Eggs usually laid in well-drained soil of marshy pastures, or in tussocks (M. Klemens, pers. commun.).

Clutch size. 1 to 8 eggs (Adler 1961), average 3 to 5.

Incubation period. 70 to 83 days.

Eggs hatch. Late August (Ernst and Barbour 1972:74) to September (Finneran 1948). Overwintering in nest may occur.

Home range/movement. Adults in a Pennsylvania marsh averaged 1.3 ac (0.5 ha) according to Ernst (1968b), moved less than 0.5 mi (0.8 km) also reported by Ernst (1968a). Females migrate outside of home range to nest (Ernst 1970).

Food habits/preferences. Omnivorous, eating crustaceans, mollusks, spiders, earthworms, aquatic insects,

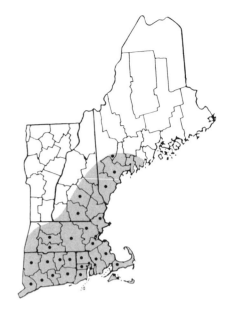

and other invertebrates; occasionally takes frogs and tadpoles, small fish, carrion, and vegetable matter. Food taken only under water.

Comments. Over-collecting, coupled with draining and filling of swamps (and possibly pollution) is depleting the population. A strongly diurnal species (Graham and Hutchinson 1979).

Selected references. Ernst 1972a; Ernst and Barbour 1972; Stewart 1974.

Bog turtle

Clemmys muhlenbergii
Testudines
Emydidae

Range. Scattered colonies in w. Connecticut, through New York, south to n.e. Maryland, s. Virginia, w. North Carolina, and Georgia.
Relative abundance. Possibly endangered; listed in Appendix 2 of the Convention on International Trade in Endangered Species of Wild Fauna and Flora, March 3, 1973, 68 Dept. of State Bull. 619 (May 14, 1973), 12 Int'l Leg. Mats. 1085 (1973).
Habitat. Unpolluted open sphagnum bogs or wet meadows; sluggish clear meadow streams with muddy or mucky bottoms (Zappalorti et al. 1979). Frequents shallow meandering waterways in swamps and wet meadows. In Connecticut associated with open canopy and calcareous wetlands (Craig 1979). Hibernates midautumn to late March or April. Hibernaculum is in a subterranean rivulet or seepage area with continually flowing water in New Jersey (Zappalorti and Farrell 1980). Commonly basks in spring and

early summer. In New Jersey bogs, individuals found basking on sedge grass tussocks or in open shallow pools (Zappalorti et al. 1979).
Special habitat requirements. Abundance of grassy or mossy cover, high humidity, and full sunlight.
Age/size at sexual maturity. At 5 years at plastron length of 75 mm (Barton and Price 1955). From 6 to 8 years, at plastron length of 70 mm (Ernst 1977).
Breeding period. Late April to early June.
Egg deposition. June to July, often in tussocks or on top of sphagnum in open, sunny areas of bogs (Zappalorti et al. 1979).
Clutch size. 2 to 5, typically 2 to 3 (Zappalorti et al. 1979).
Incubation period. 7 to 8 weeks (Nemuras 1969).
Eggs hatch. July to early September (Ernst and Barbour 1972:77–78). In northern locations hatchlings may overwinter in the nest.
Home range/movement. Average range was 1.28 ha for 19 individuals in Lancaster County, Pennsylvania (Ernst 1977). Ranging from 0.008 to 0.943 ha, traveling through wet runs

(Barton 1957 cited in Ernst 1977:246). Average movement was 12 m between recaptures for a male; when displaced, the same individual moved 0.4 km in 1 day, returning to initial point of capture (Ernst and Barbour 1972:79).
Food habits/preferences. Omnivorous, eating berries (20%), insects (80%) (Surface 1908:158); also slugs, earthworms, crayfish, frogs, snakes, nestling birds, seeds of pondweeds and sedges, snails, carrion; availability determines food consumption (Barton and Price 1955). Forages on land and under water.
Comments. Formerly named Muhlenberg's turtle. May aestivate during dry summer months (Ernst and Barbour 1972:77). Seldom active during the hottest part of the day (Zappalorti and Farrell 1980). Overcollection of this species is a problem, and locality information should be reported with discretion to prevent exploitation. Formerly abundant; population decrease related to wetland drainage and fill.
Selected references. Barton and Price 1955; Ernst and Bury 1977; Bury 1979; Zappalorti et al. 1979; Zappalorti and Farrell 1980.

Wood turtle

Clemmys insculpta
Testudines
Emydidae

Range. Nova Scotia west through the Great Lakes region to e. Minnesota. In the East extending southward to n. Virginia.

Relative abundance. Uncommon to rare (once common, populations declining).

Habitat. Slow-moving meandering streams with sandy bottoms and overhanging alders (T. Graham, pers. commun.). Basks during morning hours along banks of streams. Disperses from water sources during summer months to fields, woods, roadsides. Restricted to hardwood forest areas in New Jersey (Farrell and Zappalorti 1979). Pine barrens area, Rhode Island (Tucker, pers. observ.). Preference for lowland habitats (Strang 1983).

Returns in fall to streams to hibernate in muddy banks and bottoms through late March to April. Have been found hibernating in holes in stream banks (T. Graham, pers. commun.), in decaying vegetation of woods and trout streams with deep pools (M. Klemens, pers. commun.). Will also use abandoned muskrat burrows (Farrell and Zappalorti 1979:11). Some use same hibernaculum each year (Farrell and Zappalorti 1979).

Special habitat requirements. Wooded stream banks.

Age/size at sexual maturity. 10 years; carapace about 160 mm (J. Harding, pers. commun.).

Breeding period. March, May, October (Ernst and Barbour 1972:82), when stream temperature reaches about 15 C (Farrell and Zappalorti 1979). Mating occurs in water.

Egg deposition. May to June. Eggs laid in prepared depressions in open areas with sandy soils or gravel, not necessarily near water.

Clutch size. 4 to 12 eggs (Carr 1952:122), average 8 to 9 (Farrell and Zappalorti 1979).

Incubation period. 77 days (Allen 1955), 58 to 69 days in laboratory (Farrell and Zappalorti 1980).

Eggs hatch. August to October. Hatchlings may overwinter in the nest in northern parts of range.

Home range/movement. One male moved an average of 90 m for 3 recaptures; one female was found 15 m from initial capture point (Ernst and Barbour 1972:83). Exhibited fidelity to a particular stream or brook in New Jersey (Farrell and Zappalorti 1979), and Pennsylvania (Strang 1983); mean home range was 447 m for 10 individuals in lowland forest.

Food habits/preferences. Omnivorous, eating young vegetation, grass, moss, mushrooms, berries, insects and their larvae, worms, slugs, snails (Surface 1908:161–62); also carrion, tadpoles, frogs, and fish. Feeds in water or on land.

Comments. Formerly thought to be one of the most terrestrial turtles, actually found equally in water or on land. Lives in large groups or colonies (Farrell and Zappalorti 1979). Diurnal. Development of wooded river banks and widespread com-

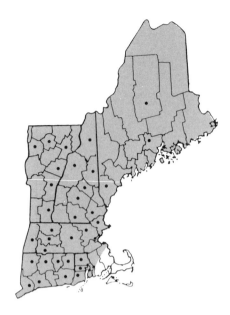

mercial collection are factors contributing to population decline. Not tolerant of pollution. Young not often encountered.

Selected references. Ernst 1972b; Farrell and Zappalorti 1979.

Eastern box turtle

Terrapene c. carolina
Testudines
Emydidae

Range. Southeastern Maine, west to the Mississippi River, central Illinois and south to n. Florida. Scattered

populations in New York.

Relative abundance. Locally common, more abundant farther south; declining in many areas.

Habitat. Woodlands, field edges, thickets, marshes, pastures, bogs, stream banks; typically found in well-drained forest bottomland (Stickel 1950). Young semiaquatic. Has been observed swimming in slow-moving streams and ponds. Found chiefly in open deciduous forests (N. Green, pers. observ.). Also found on mountain slopes in Massachusetts (T. Tyning, pers. commun.). During hot dry weather may soak in mud or water or burrow under logs or decaying vegetation for extended periods. When not active, rests in brush piles and thickets. Hibernates from depths of several inches to 2 ft (0.6 m) below surface in loose soil, decaying vegetation, mud, or in stream banks from late fall to April.

Special habitat requirements. Old fields, powerline clearings, ecotones with sandy soils favored (M. Klemens, pers. commun.).

Age/size at sexual maturity. 4 to 5 years (Ernst and Barbour 1972:43); 5 to 10 years (Minton 1972:165).

Breeding period. After emerging from hibernation in April, sometimes continuing to fall. Females may lay viable eggs for up to 4 years after mating (Ewing 1943).

Egg deposition. June to July in the Northeast. Females often seen crossing roads in Massachusetts and New Jersey during nesting season (T. Graham, pers. commun.).

Clutch size. 3 to 8 eggs, average 4 to 5.

Incubation period. 87 to 89 days (Allard 1935 cited in Carr 1952:146).

Eggs hatch. August to September, hatchlings may overwinter in nest.

Home range/movement. From 150 to 750 ft (45.7 to 228.4 m); 12 individuals averaged movement of 390 ft

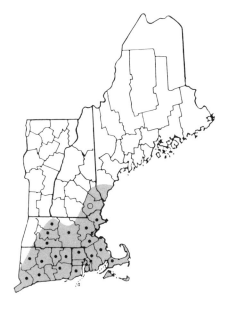

(118.8 m) on Long Island (Breder 1927). For 62 individuals in mixed woodlands and open habitat on Long Island average range was less than 750 ft (228.4 m) as reported by Nichols (1939). Mean of 167 m in mixed woodlands in Pennsylvania (Strang 1983). Stickel (1950) reported average diameter of 350 ft (106.6 m) in Maryland. One individual was found within 0.25 mi (0.4 km) from point of release 60 years previously (Allen 1868 cited in Babcock 1919:412). Maintains same home range for many years; occasionally leaves normal home range for random wandering or egg laying (Stickel 1950). Homing instinct displayed by 45 out of 60 turtles (Nichols 1939).

Food habits/preferences. Younger individuals chiefly carnivorous, older individuals more herbivorous. Food items include animals such as earthworms, slugs, snails, insects and their larvae, particularly grasshoppers, moths, and beetles; crayfish, frogs, toads, snakes, and carrion; vegetable matter such as leaves, grass, bugs, berries, fruits, and fungi.

Comments. Terrestrial and diurnal. Digs into leaf litter toward end of day. Bisection of habitat by roads can reduce or destroy populations. The reversion of much agricultural land to woodland may be a beneficial change to populations (M. Klemens, pers. commun.). Estimated age at full growth is 20 years. May live 60 to 80 years (Nichols 1939). Some individuals may live over 100 years (Graham and Hutchinson 1969).

Selected references. Stickel 1950; Carr 1952; Ernst and Barbour 1972.

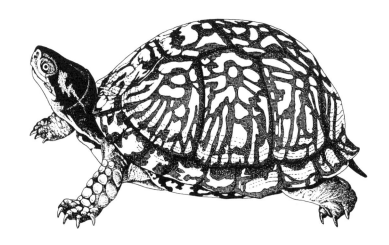

Map turtle

Graptemys geographica
Testudines
Emydidae

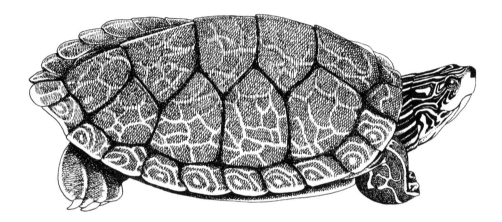

Range. Lake Champlain to the Great Lakes west to the Mississippi drainage to e. Minnesota, south to Louisiana and n.w. Georgia. Along Susquehanna drainage. Introduced into

Delaware River. Nests as far south as Poughkeepsie, Dutchess County, New York.

Relative abundance. Uncommon and of limited distribution.

Habitat. Rivers and lakes. Aquatic, it prefers large bodies of water with soft bottoms and aquatic vegetation. Hibernates in mud of shallow water from late fall to early spring. May be active on or under ice. Gregariously basks on logs and rocks or along beaches and grassy shores. In Michigan found in riffles of pebble-bottom streams that have interspersed, deeper, muddier pools (M. Klemens, pers. commun.). Moves from shallow bays to nesting areas and reenters bays to overwinter in Quebec (Gordon 1980).

Special habitat requirements. Water bodies with muddy or soft bottom substrate.

Age/size at sexual maturity. Females at 7.5 in (190.5 mm) and larger (New-

man 1906 cited in Pope 1939:169).

Breeding period. April and autumn (Ernst and Barbour 1972:110).

Egg deposition. May to July, peak mid-June. Nesting season begins in mid-June in Quebec and averages 2 weeks in duration (Gordon 1980). Nests made in soft sand or soil away from beaches.

Clutch size. 10 to 16 (Cahn 1937), typically 12 to 14 eggs. More than one clutch may be laid.

Eggs hatch. Late August to early September (Carr 1952:199); some may overwinter in the nest.

Home range/movement. Unreported.

Food habits/preferences. Aquatic feeders—snails and clams are the major components of the diet; other small mollusks, crayfish, vegetable matter, fish, insects, and carrion are eaten (Carr 1952:199).

Selected references. Newman 1906; Evermann and Clarke 1916.

Red-eared slider

Pseudemys scripta elegans
Testudines
Emydidae

Range. Central Ohio west to s.e. Iowa, south into New Mexico, Texas, Alabama, and w. Tennessee. Released and established in parts of Massachusetts and Connecticut.
Relative abundance. Locally common.
Habitat. Ponds, shallow areas of lakes, creeks, and drainage ditches. Hibernates when water temperature drops below 10 C. Sometimes occupies muskrat burrows or hollow stumps.
Special habitat requirements. Quiet water with muddy bottom, abundant vegetation, projecting substrate, such as logs or rocks for basking.
Age/size at sexual maturity. Determined by size rather than age: plastron length for males 90 to 100 mm, for females 150 to 195 mm.
Breeding period. Unreported.

Egg deposition. April to mid-July. Females may be capable of reproducing for 40 to 50 years. Average longevity may be 50 to 75 years (Cagle 1950). Female excavates nest hole in earth, deposits eggs, and seals hole with mud and debris. May move a mile (1.6 km) from water to find suitable nest site.
Clutch size. 2 to 22, typically 5 to 10 eggs; 1 to 3 clutches per season.
Incubation period. 68 to 70 days (*Pseudemys scripta troostii* incubated in laboratory, Cagle 1950).
Eggs hatch. July 1 to mid-September (Illinois and Louisiana).
Home range/movement. Most sliders (n = 1,006) inhabiting a drainage ditch in Mississippi River flood plain remained within one-half mile (0.8 km) of release site (Cagle 1944:24).
Food habits/preferences. Omnivorous, taking tadpoles, crayfish, mollusks, large larvae of aquatic insects, small fish (Cahn 1937).
Comments. Possibly feral in Maryland (Cooper 1959). Active from late April until October in Illinois. High-

ly aquatic, avoids land except when laying eggs. Aestivates in mud when temperatures exceed 31 C (Cagle 1950). Common name is now the common slider and the preferred genus name is *Trachemys* (T. Tyning, pers. commun.).
Selected references. Cahn 1937; Cagle 1950; Cooper 1959; Webb 1961.

Plymouth redbelly turtle

Pseudemys rubriventris bangsi
Testudines
Emydidae

Range. Plymouth County, Massachusetts. Skeletal remains and a shell have been found recently in Ipswich, Essex County (Graham 1982).

Relative abundance. Endangered (federal list).

Habitat. Ponds of different sizes in Plymouth County. Frequents shallow coves (Graham 1971a).

Special habitat requirements. Muddy-bottomed shallows with abundant aquatic vegetation, especially milfoil *(Myriophyllum)* and bladderwort *(Utricularia)* (Graham 1980).

Age/size at sexual maturity. Probably not reached during first 9 years (Graham 1971a). Average life span estimated at 40 to 55 years (Graham 1980).

Breeding period. Probably early spring and fall (T. Graham, pers. commun.).

Egg deposition. Mid-June to early July. Prefer to nest in disturbed sites (T. Graham, pers. commun.).

Clutch size. Range 12 to 17 eggs, average 14.5 (Graham, ms.).

Eggs hatch. September to October (T. Graham, pers. commun.). Average hatching time of 75 days for 17 eggs hatched in a laboratory at 25 C (Graham 1971b). If hatchlings overwinter in the nest, they emerge the following July.

Home range/movement. Unknown but wanders on land especially during fall and late spring. Found 0.5 to 2.0 mi (0.8 to 3.2 km) from water on occasion. Significance of wandering unknown (Graham, ms.).

Food habits/preferences. Primarily herbivorous, feeding mainly on milfoil, also feeds on bladderwort (Graham 1980) and arrowhead *(Sagittaria)* (Graham 1971a). Dietary shift to crayfish in fourth season (Graham 1971a).

Comments. Basks during early morning hours on elevated sites or in water by floating or resting on weed mats (Graham 1980). Discovered in Plymouth, Massachusetts, in 1869 (Lucas 1916). Population estimate of 200 to 300 in Plymouth County (T. Graham, pers. commun.).

Selected references. Graham 1971a, 1971b, 1980; Lazell 1976a.

Eastern painted turtle

Chrysemys p. picta
Testudines
Emydidae

Range. Nova Scotia to n.e. New York, south to Cape Hatteras and in-

land to e. Alabama. In the Northeast intergrades with the midland painted turtle.

Relative abundance. Common, often abundant.

Habitat. Quiet shallow ponds, marshes, woodland pools, rivers, lake shores, wet meadows, bogs, slow-moving streams. Sometimes in brackish tidal waters, salt marshes (Pope 1939:183). Stagnant and polluted waters are sometimes inhabited (Smith 1956:150). When in water, usually remains in submerged vegetation. Basks on small hummocks, logs, rocks, sometimes congregating in large groups. Hibernates by burrowing into mud or decayed vegetation of pond bottoms.

Special habitat requirements. Aquatic habitat.

Age/size at sexual maturity. Correlated with size; in Michigan males exceeded 81 mm plastron length, females ranged from 110 to 120 mm (Gibbons 1968a).

Breeding period. March to mid-June and fall (Gibbons 1968a). Peak in April in Connecticut (Carr 1952:218).

Egg deposition. May to July. Nest sites within a few yards of water

(Cahn 1937 cited in Smith 1961:140), or up to one half mile (0.8 km) away (T. Tyning, pers. commun.).

Clutch size. 2 to 11. Females may lay 2 clutches (Gibbons 1968a), typically 5 to 6.

Incubation period. 72 to 80 days (Ernst and Barbour 1972:143). 63 days (Lynn and vonBrand 1945). Hatchlings from late clutches may overwinter in the nest. Nests are often destroyed by raccoons and skunks.

Eggs hatch. Late August to early September in Connecticut (Finneran 1948).

Home range/movement. Displays short-distance homing ability; fewer than 15% moved more than 100 m in a marsh in Michigan (Gibbons 1968a). Average distance traveled was 112 m in a shallow bay of a Wisconsin lake; 70% of the turtles did not travel. Individuals may remain in the same locality for years if conditions are favorable (Pearse 1923).

Food habits/preferences. Aquatic insects, snails, small fish, tadpoles, mussels, carrion, and aquatic plants taken by foraging along the bottom. Diet usually about 50% vegetation.

Comments. Diurnal. Emerges from

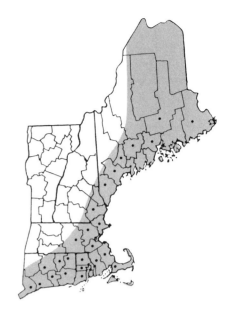

hibernation in late March or early April in Massachusetts (Graham 1971a).

Chrysemys p. picta and *C. p. marginata* intergrade in the Northeast. Intergrades accounted for 79% of 89 individuals examined from the Delaware Water Gap in New Jersey (Stein 1980).

Selected references. Carr 1952; Gibbons 1968a; Ernst 1971; Ernst and Barbour 1972.

Midland painted turtle

Chrysemys picta marginata
Testudines
Emydidae

Range. New Hampshire, s. Quebec and Ontario to e. Wisconsin. Through central Illinois south to Tennessee. Vermont and New York south to west of the Shenandoah River.

Relative abundance. Intergrades with *C. p. picta* are abundant.

Habitat. Quiet water, preferably shallow areas with dense vegeta-

tion. Tolerant of some industrial pollution. Basks in groups on sunlit logs. Sometimes found away from water. Usually hibernates in muddy bottoms of ponds but has been reported active yearlong.

Special habitat requirements. Aquatic habitats.

Age/size at sexual maturity. 5 years for males, 6 to 7 years for females (Pope 1939:185).

Breeding period. Early spring after emerging from hibernation; fall matings have been reported.

Egg deposition. June to July. Eggs often laid in high banks.

Clutch size. 3 to 10 eggs, average 5 to 8.

Eggs hatch. Hatchlings emerge in September or the next spring (Smith 1961:140).

Home range/movement. Average summer diurnal movement within a pond, about 90 m. Movements have been divided into three types: initial emigration in the spring of 63 to 144 m from hibernation ponds to other ponds with floating mats of vegetation; late summer movements of 86

to 91 m, back to hibernation ponds; and late autumn movements of 88 to 130 m to deep-water areas in Michigan (Sexton 1959). 60% of individuals studied in a Michigan lake exhibited homing behavior (Williams 1952).

Food habits/preferences. Aquatic vascular plants, seeds, algae, and invertebrates including crustaceans, mollusks, insects and their larvae, and worms. Also takes carrion, fish, and frogs. Aquatic plants comprised more than 60% of the diet and insects about 20% in Michigan (Lagler 1943).

Comments. In New England, there are no midland turtle populations; subspecies intergrades with *C. p. picta.* Information provided in this account is based on references for *C. p. marginata* where intergrades do not occur. In New England, *C. p. marginata* and *C. p. picta* life history and habitat information are the same (M. Klemens, pers. commun.).

Selected references. Carr 1952; Sexton 1959; Smith 1961.

Blanding's turtle

Emydoidea blandingii
Testudines
Emydidae

Range. Scattered colonies in New York, New Hampshire, and e. Massachusetts. Escaped individuals found in Connecticut (Lamson 1935). Southern Quebec across the Lake States to central Minnesota, south to Iowa and central Illinois. Spotted occurrence from Nova Scotia to Ohio.

Relative abundance. Populations localized and distribution spotty throughout its range (McCoy 1973:136.1). Generally scarce to rare, locally abundant in Massachusetts (Lazell 1972). An endangered species in Canada.

Habitat. Shallow waters preferred; marshes, bogs, ditches, ponds, swamps, also in protected coves and inlets of large lakes, oxbows, and pools adjacent to rivers, with abundant aquatic vegetation. May wander overland. Basks on logs, stumps, banks. Active in winter or hibernates in mud or debris.

Special habitat requirements. Shallow waters with soft muddy bottoms and aquatic vegetation.

Age/size at sexual maturity. During twelfth year for males with a plastron length of 181 to 190 mm, Massachusetts (Graham and Doyle 1977); males 131 to 190 mm in Michigan (Gibbons 1968b). Size differences between these two populations probably due to differences in food quality and availability (Graham and Doyle 1977).

Breeding period. Early spring through October, most often from March to May (Ernst and Barbour 1972:181). Peak in late April (Graham and Depain, ms.).

Egg deposition. June to July. Nests made in sandy soils of upland areas.

Clutch size. 6 to 11 eggs (Carr 1952:136), typically 8 to 9 eggs, clutches of 9, 13, and 16 eggs for Massachusetts females (Graham and Depain, ms). Clutch of 17 for a July nesting female (Graham and Doyle 1979). Two clutches may be laid each season.

Incubation period. Unreported.

Eggs hatch. Autumn or next spring.

Home range/movement. Less than 100 m for 4 individuals in a marsh in s.w. Michigan (Gibbons 1968b).

Food habits/preferences. Crustaceans, insects, mollusks, fish, carrion, aquatic plants, succulent shoots, and berries. Crustaceans and crayfish comprise about 50% of diet, insects over 25%, and other invertebrates and vegetable matter 25% (Lagler 1943).

Comments. Primarily diurnal. In Michigan, found in rivers (M. Klemens, pers. commun.).

Selected references. Gibbons 1968b; McCoy 1973; Graham and Doyle 1977, 1979.

Eastern spiny softshell

Trionyx s. spiniferus
Testudines
Trionychidae

Range. Western New York across the Great Lakes States to the Mississippi River, n. Wisconsin south to the Tennessee River extending east to central Pennsylvania. A disjunct colony occupies the Champlain Valley. Introduced into the Maurice River system of New Jersey.

Relative abundance. Uncommon.

Habitat. Large river systems; also lakes and ponds. Intolerant of pollution from sewage, industrial or chemical wastes (Minton 1972:191). Basks on sand bars, mud flats, and grassy beaches but will use logs, rocks, and other objects when sandy or muddy banks are not available (Williams and Christiansen 1982). Aquatic, it hibernates beneath 2 to 3 in (5.1 to 7.6 cm) of river-bottom mud from October to April in the North.

Special habitat requirements. Shallow muddy bottoms for burrowing. Some aquatic vegetation essential (N. Green, pers. observ.).

Age/size at sexual maturity. Females with plastron length of 180 to 200 mm, males, 90 to 100 mm.

Breeding period. April or May.

Egg deposition. May to August. Eggs laid in sandy soil or gravel beds near water's edge.

Clutch size. Typically 12 to 18, with a range of 4 to 32 eggs (Ernst and Barbour 1972:264).

Eggs hatch. August to October or hatchlings overwinter in nest.

Home range/movement. Unreported.

Food habits/preferences. Chiefly carnivorous. Crayfish and insects are the major food items with tadpoles, frogs, mollusks, and fish eaten less frequently; vegetation and other plant materials also consumed. Primarily benthic feeders (Williams and Christiansen 1982).

Comments. Somewhat nocturnal.

Selected references. Ernst and Barbour 1972; Minton 1972; Webb 1973.

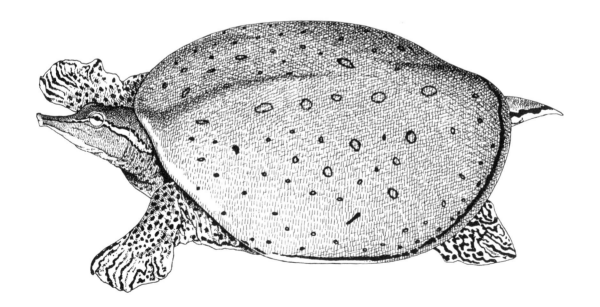

Lizards
(order Squamata,
suborder Lacertilia)

The sole New England lizard is a skink (family Scincidae). Skinks have long cylindrical bodies and tails, and smooth, unkeeled, sleek scales. They are diurnal and most species are insectivorous (Behler and King 1979:570).

Five-lined skink

Eumeces fasciatus
Squamata, Lacertilia
Scincidae

Range. Southern end of Lake George, New York, and s.e. New York south to n. Florida, west to central Texas. Northern limit from Pennsylvania, Ontario to central Wisconsin and n. Missouri.

Relative abundance. Rare in the Northeast through s.e. Connecticut, peripheral in New Jersey. Common in Pennsylvania, Maryland, and West Virginia. Formerly reported in the Albany Pine Bush of New York (Stewart and Rossi 1981). Records for Massachusetts are from Barre (Storer 1840:19) and New Bedford (Allen 1870:260).

Habitat. Mesic wooded areas, open or moderately dense with ground cover. Most abundant around old buildings and open woods. Frequently in damp spots, under logs, rock piles, leaf litter, sawdust piles. Suns for brief periods on warm days (Smith 1946:349). Found on open talus slopes in mixed deciduous woodlands, New York. Primarily terrestrial but will climb snags to find insects. Hibernates from October until mid-March in decaying logs or below the frost line, underground or under large rocks.

Special habitat requirements. Open woods with logs and slash piles.

Age/size at sexual maturity. After second hibernation.

Breeding period. May.

Egg deposition. Typically in June or July, 6 to 7 weeks after breeding (Smith 1956:193). Eggs laid under rocks, logs, in rotted stumps, in loose soil. Females usually guard eggs during the incubation period (Conant 1975:122) and will ingest addled eggs; it has been suggested that brooding females remove these eggs to reduce chances of predation (Groves 1982).

Clutch size. 4 to 20 eggs (Barbour 1971:209), typically 9 to 12. Younger individuals lay fewer eggs (Fitch 1970).

Incubation period. Approximately 1 month (Vogt 1981:121).

Home range/movement. Males home range diameter about 90 ft (27.4 m), females about 30 ft (9.1 m), in e. Kansas (Fitch 1954 cited in Minton 1972:210). Individuals may remain in same home range or move after emerging from hibernation.

Food habits/preferences. Primarily insects and spiders, also snails, grubs, small vertebrates including young mice. Lizards occasionally eaten; will eat its own shed skin.

Comments. Tail autotomy is an effective means of distracting predators. The detached tail actively writhes, generally allowing the lizard to escape. Regenerated tails are not usually as long as the original.

Selected references. Smith 1946, 1956; Barbour 1971.

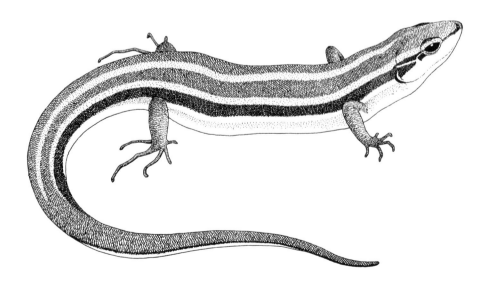

Snakes
(Order Squamata,
suborder Serpentes)

Of eleven families of snakes worldwide, five are represented in the United States and Canada, two of which are in New England: the Colubridae and Viperidae. Snakes are the most numerous group of reptiles in New England; sixteen species and subspecies are found within the area. Of these, the maritime garter snake *(Thamnophis sirtalis pallidula)* is the only subspecies that does not occur further south. The timber rattlesnake *(Crotalus horridus)*, northern copperhead *(Agkistrodon contortrix mokeson)*, eastern hognose *(Heterodon platyrhinos)*, ribbon *(Thamnophis s. sauritus)*, worm *(Carphophis a. amoenus)*, and milk *(Lampropeltis t. triangulum)* snakes, the northern brown *(Storeria d. dekayi)* and water *(Nerodia s. sipedon)* snakes, the northern black racer *(Coluber c. constrictor)*, and the black rat snake *(Elaphe o. obsoleta)* reach their northeastern range limits in New England.

Snakes are distinctive in having elongated bodies with scaly skins and in having no limbs, external ear openings, or eyelids. All snakes are carnivorous (in the broadest sense—they eat animal prey, although many are primarily insectivorous, some are piscivorous, and so on) and all swallow their prey whole. Snakes, like all reptiles, continue to grow throughout their lives.

Snakes either lay eggs or bear live young. The terms *oviparous, ovoviviparous,* and *viviparous* have been used to describe reproductive modes. These terms have been applied loosely, and the result has been more confusion than enlightenment. Oviparous species lay eggs. The eggs of ovoviviparous species hatch within the female or hatch immediately upon extrusion from the cloaca. Viviparous species bear live young (McFarland

1979:505). We will use the terms *oviparous* for species that lay eggs and *viviparous* for those that bear live young.

The Colubridae is the largest snake family and contains a great diversity of species, including semi-aquatic, fossorial, arboreal, and terrestrial forms. In all, the head is at least as wide as the neck, and the belly scales extend across the width of the body. All nonpoisonous New England snakes are colubrids (Behler and King 1979:589).

The Viperidae or pit vipers are represented by two genera in New England—*Agkistrodon* (copperheads and cottonmouths) and *Crotalus* (one of two rattlesnake genera) —each containing a single species in our area.

Both species are heavy-bodied snakes with heads that are conspicuously wider than their necks. They are boldly patterned with cross bands or blotches. A heat-sensing pit, used for locating warm-blooded prey, is located on each side of the head between the eye and nostril. The eyes have vertical pupils. The rattlesnake bears a unique tail structure of flattened, interlocking horny segments that produce a buzz when shaken. One segment is added each time the skin is shed, which normally occurs several times during the year (Behler and King 1979:682).

Northern water snake
Nerodia s. sipedon
Squamata, Serpentes
Colubridae

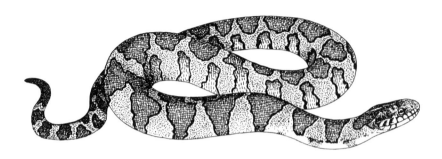

Range. Southern Maine, s. Ontario to n. Wisconsin, south through Kansas to e. Colorado, n. Oklahoma to central Indiana, Kentucky, and Tennessee, east to North Carolina and New England.

Relative abundance. Abundant in suitable habitat.

Habitat. Aquatic and semiaquatic. Common around spillways and bridges where rocks provide cover. Uncommon in deeply shaded woodland swamps and ponds, probably due to lack of basking sites (M. Klemens, pers. commun.). Found in the vicinity of rivers, brooks, wet meadows, ponds, swamps, bogs, old quarries. Inhabits salt or fresh water (Wright and Wright 1957:513), absent from heavily polluted waters. Prefers still or slow-moving water. Hibernates in crevices of rocky ledges or in banks adjacent to water habitat.

Special habitat requirements. Branches or logs overhanging the water, or boulders of dams and causeways in

reservoirs (T. Tyning, pers. commun.).

Age/size at sexual maturity. Males 635 to 1,148 mm, females 650 to 1,295 mm (Wright and Wright 1957:513).

Breeding period. April to May and early fall.

Young born. August to early October, usually during the last half of August. Viviparous.

No. young. 10 to 76, average 20 to 40. Larger females have larger litters.

Home range/movement. One individual moved 380 ft (115.8 m) along a river after 2 years (Stickel and Cope 1947). In large ponds at an Indiana fish hatchery, 80 % were recaptured in the same pond, 89 % were in the same pond or an adjacent pond. Snakes along streams had larger home ranges (Fraker 1970).

Food habits/preferences. Opportunistic consumer of cold-blooded vertebrates: fish comprise 61 % of food items, frogs and toads 21 %, salamanders 12 %; also insects, crayfish, recently dead fish (Uhler et al. 1939).

Fish comprise over 95 % of diet (Raney and Roecker 1947). May occasionally take shrews and mice. Diet varies greatly according to food availability.

Comments. Frequently found basking. Active both day and night.

Selected references. Schmidt and Davis 1941; Wright and Wright 1957.

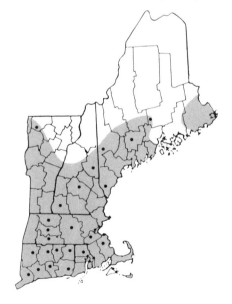

Northern brown snake

Storeria d. dekayi
Squamata, Serpentes
Colubridae

Range. Eastern United States from s. Maine and s. Canada west to Michigan, south to South Carolina. Range overlaps that of the midland brown snake.

Relative abundance. Common.

Habitat. Ubiquitous. Urban and rural areas, dry or moist situations, vacant lots, parks, trash piles. May be abundant along railroad tracks (T. Tyning, pers. commun.). In the wild, found in damp woods, swamps, clearings, bogs, roadsides, open fields. Hides under stones, banks, logs, brush piles, leaves. Rare in old growth forests (J. Lazell, pers. commun.). Hibernates in large groups from October to November until March or April; may use ant hills or abandoned mammal burrows.

Age/size at sexual maturity. 2 years (Noble and Clausen 1936).

Breeding period. Late March to April and possibly in the fall.

Young born. Late July to August. (Wright and Wright 1957:701). Gestation period of 105 to 113 days (Fitch 1970). Viviparous.

No. young. 3 to 27 young (Fitch 1970), typically 14.

Home range/movement. Average daily movement of 10 to 15 ft (3.0 to 4.6 m) on Long Island. Thirteen of 32 individuals displayed homing behavior (Noble and Clausen 1936).

Food habits/preferences. Slugs, snails, earthworms, insects, minnows, and tiny toads are occasionally eaten.

Comments. Formerly DeKay's snake. Commonly found in aggregations throughout the year (Noble and Clausen 1936). May appear to be scarce during July and August when it moves down into soil to lower temperature zones. Degree of fossorial tendency varies with microhabitat temperature preference

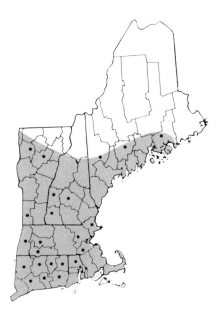

(Elick et al. 1979). Active evening to early morning; one of the few New England snakes that is active at night.

Selected references. Schmidt and Davis 1941; Wright and Wright 1957.

Northern redbelly snake

Storeria o. occipitomaculata
Squamata, Serpentes
Colubridae

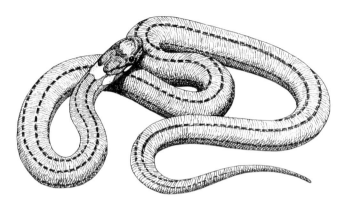

Range. Nova Scotia to s. Manitoba, south to e. Texas, Georgia, and throughout the e. United States.
Relative abundance. Locally abundant.
Habitat. Moist woods, hillsides, sphagnum bogs, upland meadows and valleys. Found under surface debris, also around abandoned buildings. Occurs at elevations from

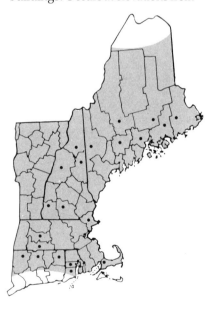

sea level to mountains. Prefers woodlands: pine, oak-hickory, aspen, hemlock groves (Wright and Wright 1957:717). More frequently found in upland woody ridges. Occasionally found in damp meadows, marshy areas, swamp and bog edges. Hibernates from fall to March or April. Active through mid-October in Connecticut (M. Klemens, pers. commun.).
Special habitat requirements. Woodlands.
Age/size at sexual maturity. Males 182 to 359 mm, females 211 to 383 mm (Wright and Wright 1957:718); at 2 years (Blanchard 1937a).
Breeding period. Probably after emerging from hibernation; a late summer or fall mating may also occur (Barbour 1971:287).
Young born. August to September. Viviparous.
No. young. 1 to 14 young (Blanchard 1937a), typically 7 to 8.
Home range/movement. One adult was found 100 ft (30.4 m) from release point in Michigan after 7 days (Blanchard 1937a).

Food habits/preferences. Consumes slugs, earthworms, soft insects and larvae, sowbugs; occasionally small salamanders.
Comments. Has been found active at all times of day and evening. Degree of fossorial behavior varies (Elick et al. 1979). Young commonly mistaken for young ring-neck or northern brown snakes.
Selected references. Schmidt and Davis 1941; Wright and Wright 1957; Barbour 1971.

Eastern garter snake

Thamnophis s. sirtalis
Squamata, Serpentes
Colubridae

Range. Nova Scotia to e. Manitoba south to e. Texas, and throughout the e. United States. Intergradation with range of *T. s. pallidula* occurs in n. New England (Fitch 1980:270.1).
Relative abundance. Very abundant; most common and widespread snake.
Habitat. Ubiquitous, terrestrial. Moist areas, forest edges, stream edges, fence rows, vacant lots, bogs, swamps, overgrown yards. One specimen found under a rock in a stream flowing through a dark hemlock grove (M. Klemens, pers. commun.). Found in almost all damp environments, from river bottoms to high mountain elevations.

Hibernates, often gregariously, in holes, rock crevices, mud, anthills, rotted wood, uprooted trees, house foundations, and sometimes partially or completely submerged under stream-bed rocks, from October to March or April. One of the earliest snakes to emerge from hibernation. Can survive the winter above frost line (Bailey 1949).

Age/size at sexual maturity. Females in second year, some males the second spring after birth (Carpenter 1952a). At 400 mm snout to vent length for males and 500 mm for females in Kansas (Fitch 1965:531).
Breeding period. Concentrated in the first few warm days after emergence from hibernation in mid-March to May, also in fall before hibernation (Anderson 1965:169). Breeds at or near hibernation site.
Young born. July to early September. Gestation period of 3 to 4 months or longer in cooler climates (Blanchard and Blanchard 1942). Viviparous.
No. young. 3 to 85 young, typically 14 to 40. Zehr (1962) found 12 to 13 young was the average in New Hampshire. Number of young correlated with size and age of female (Fitch 1965:558).
Home range/movement. Approximately 5 ac (2.0 ha), most ranges were smaller in cut-over agricultural fields in Indiana. Range about 2 ac (0.8 ha) in Michigan woodlands and open fields (Carpenter 1952a). Home ranges of 35.0 ac (14 ha) for males and 22.2 ac (9.1 ha) for females were found in mixed habitat in Kansas (Fitch 1965:538). Many individuals migrate from hibernacula to summer ranges.

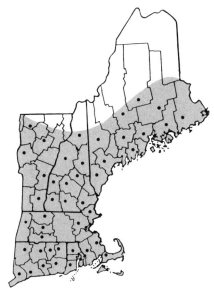

Food habits/preferences. Earthworms comprise 80% of food items. Also amphibians, carrion, fish, leeches, caterpillars, other insects, small birds, rodents (Carpenter 1952b); slugs, other snakes, mollusks, crayfish, sowbugs (Hamilton 1951).
Comments. Diurnal but sometimes active at night (Minton 1972:250). Seeks cover under objects on hot summer days. Pesticides have reduced local populations in New York (Gochfeld 1975).
Selected references. Carpenter 1952b; Wright and Wright 1957; Fitch 1965, 1980.

Maritime garter snake

Thamnophis sirtalis pallidula
Squamata, Serpentes
Colubridae

Range. Eastern Quebec extending to Alberta in discontinuous populations, south to n. New Hampshire, New York, and n. Michigan. Intergrades with *T. s. sirtalis* to west and south.

Relative abundance. Unreported.

Habitat. Found in mature northern hardwood stands, fir stands with mixed understory, and along forest roads in northern New Hampshire.

Comments. Little information available on life history.

Selected references. Bleakney 1959; Fitch 1980.

Eastern ribbon snake

Thamnophis s. sauritus
Squamata, Serpentes
Colubridae

Range. Southern Maine to South Carolina and the Florida panhandle. Southern Indiana south to e. Louisiana. Northern limits through s. Indiana to central New England.
Relative abundance. Generally common, but uncommon in Connecticut (M. Klemens, pers. commun.).
Habitat. Stream edges, swampy areas, wet meadows, ponds, bogs, ditches. Semiaquatic, it prefers areas with brushy vegetation at water's edge for concealment. Also in damp or wet deciduous or northern pine forests. Seldom far from cover (Carpenter 1952b). May escape higher ground temperatures in summer by seeking shelter in shrubs or underground. Hibernates from October to March (Wright and Wright 1957:825).
Special habitat requirements. Mesic woodlands with aquatic habitat.
Age/size at sexual maturity. Females during second year (Carpenter

1952a), males 400 to 819 mm, females 451 to 900 mm (Wright and Wright 1957:825).
Breeding period. After emergence from hibernation.
Young born. Late July to September. Viviparous.
No. young. 3 to 20, typically 10 to 12.
Home range/movement. Average activity range of about 2 ac (0.8 ha), average distance traveled was approximately 280 ft (85.3 m) in open Michigan grassland and marsh (Carpenter 1952b).
Food habits/preferences. Frogs, toads, and salamanders comprise 90 % of prey items; usually smaller or metamorphosing individuals were taken; also mice, spiders, minnows, and some insects (Carpenter 1952b).
Selected references. Carpenter 1952b; Rossman 1970.

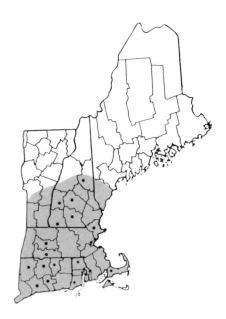

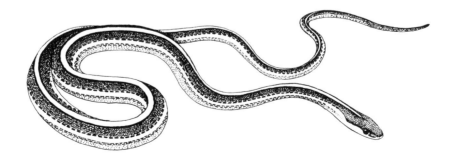

Northern ribbon snake

Thamnophis sauritus septentrionalis
Squamata, Serpentes
Colubridae

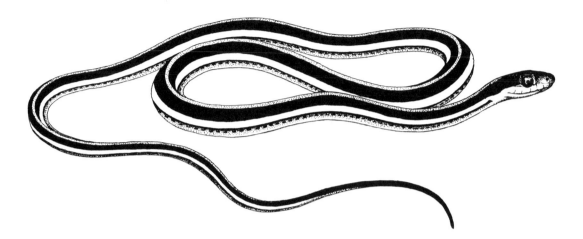

Range. Central Maine west through
n.w. New England and s. Ontario to
Michigan, south to s.e. Illinois, Indiana, Ohio, and n. Pennsylvania.
Relative abundance. Rare.
Habitat. Sunny areas with low,
dense vegetation that are near bodies of shallow quiet water. Damp
meadows, grassy marshes, northern sphagnum bogs, borders of
ponds, lakes, and meandering
creeks. Semiaquatic. Probably hibernates October to March (Minton
1972:260).
Special habitat requirements. Shallow,
permanent water in open, grassy
habitat.
Age/size at sexual maturity. Some females at almost 2 years (Carpenter
1952a).
Breeding period. Probably spring and
fall (Minton 1972:260).
Young born. July to August (Minton
1972:260).
No. young. 4 to 10 or 11 young (Minton 1972:260). Viviparous.
Home range/movement. Unknown.

Food habits/preferences. Frogs, salamanders, fish. Captives will eat
minnows. Brown (1979) notes that
93 % of the food items in the stom-
achs of 21 specimens were comprised of anurans.
Comments. Diurnal.
Selected references. Minton 1972;
Conant 1975.

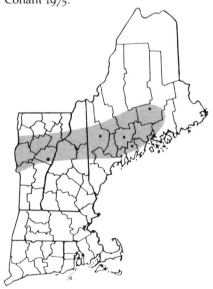

Eastern hognose snake

Heterodon platyrhinos
Squamata, Serpentes
Colubridae

Range. Cape Cod and central Massachusetts west to Ohio, s. Ontario, central Minnesota, and s.e. South Dakota, south to central Texas and s. Florida.

Relative abundance. Locally common.

Habitat. Where sandy soils predominate, such as beaches, open fields, dry, open pine, or deciduous woods. Has been found on hillsides, farm fields, and around outbuildings. In Pennsylvania most frequently found in upland situations, intermountain and river valleys (McCoy and Bianculli 1966). Low-lying areas of Connecticut (M. Klemens, pers. commun.), and in marshy woodlands in the Albany Pine Bush in New York, and wooded creek bottomlands (M. Stewart, pers. commun.). Hibernates from late September to April or May under forest floor debris, stumps, trash piles (Wright and Wright 1957:308).

Special habitat requirements. Sandy soils, open woodlands.

Age/size at sexual maturity. Males 400 to 1,050 mm, females 450 to 1,200 mm (Wright and Wright 1957:309).

Breeding period. April to May, and probably fall (Fitch 1970).

Egg deposition. June to July. Eggs laid in earth, under or in pulpy wood of decaying logs.

Clutch size. 4 to 61 eggs, typically 22 (Fitch 1970).

Incubation period. 39 to 60 days (Anderson 1965:185).

Eggs hatch. July to September, peak in August.

Home range/movement. After 5 months one individual in Maryland mixed habitat had moved 100 ft (30 m) (Stickel and Cope 1947).

Food habits/preferences. Toads preferred, but frogs, fish, salamanders, insects, and worms are taken; rarely small birds and mammals and occasionally other snakes (Edgren 1955). Amphibians and reptiles comprised 80 % of the food items in 10 specimens in Virginia (Uhler et al. 1939).

Comments. Diurnal. Fossorial habits, probably seeks cover by burrowing

(Edgren 1955). Particularly vulnerable to heavy herbicide and pesticide use. Defense behavior includes feigning death, mock striking and head rearing, and "hood" display.

Selected references. Edgren 1955; Smith 1956; Wright and Wright 1957; McCoy and Bianculli 1966; Blem 1981.

Northern ringneck snake
Diadophis punctatus edwardsi
Squamata, Serpentes
Colubridae

Range. Nova Scotia, s. Ontario to Wisconsin. Eastern and s. Ohio to s.e. Illinois, n.e. Alabama and north through central Virginia to New England.

Relative abundance. Common.

Habitat. Found under cover especially in moist shady woodlands with abundant hiding material: stony woodland pastures, rocks, stone walls, old woodland junk piles, logs, debris, loose bark of logs and stumps; shale banks in Maine (Fowler and Sutcliffe 1952), and boards are all used. Hibernates from September to April or May. One individual found in a woodchuck den (Grizzel 1949).

Special habitat requirements. Mesic areas with abundant cover.

Age/size at sexual maturity. Males at 13 to 14 months (Fitch 1960b), males 220 to 500 mm, females 220 to 550

mm (Wright and Wright 1957:187).

Breeding period. Soon after emerging from hibernation.

Egg deposition. Late June to early July. Eggs laid in rotted logs, under logs or stones. Several females may use the same nest.

Clutch size. 1 to 10 eggs, typically 3 or 4 (Blanchard 1937b). Smaller females lay fewer eggs (Fitch 1970).

Incubation period. 4 to 6 weeks (Minton 1944). Average of 56 days in laboratory conditions (Blanchard 1930 cited in Wright and Wright 1957:188).

Eggs hatch. Late August through September.

Home range/movement. Undocumented.

Food habits/preferences. Toads, frogs, salamanders, earthworms, lizards, small snakes, insects, grubs.

Comments. Secretive and nocturnal. Degree of fossorial tendency varies

with temperature preference (Elick et al. 1979).

Selected references. Schmidt and Davis 1941; Wright and Wright 1957.

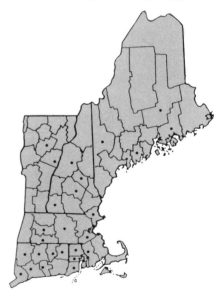

Eastern worm snake

Carphophis a. amoenus
Squamata, Serpentes
Colubridae

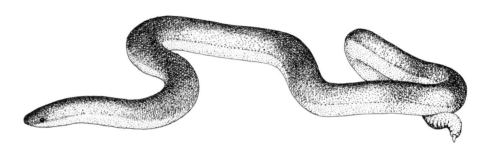

Range. Southcentral Massachusetts, s.e. New York through central Pennsylvania to s. Ohio. South to central Alabama, n. Georgia, and South Carolina.

Relative abundance. Locally abundant.

Habitat. Dry to moist forests, often near streams; in the loose soil of gardens or weedy pastures. Sandy areas favored (M. Klemens, pers. commun.). Found in dry oak–pitch pine areas in Springfield, Massachusetts (T. Tyning, pers. commun.) and under loose bark slabs, logs, stones, leaves, other debris. Hibernates in rotting wood, underground, or in burrows of other animals. Remains underground until May except on warm sunny days.

Special habitat requirements. Loose soil for burrowing; cover objects.

Age/size at sexual maturity. 3 years (Fitch 1970).

Breeding period. Probably spring to early summer (McCauley 1945:97) and fall (Fitch 1970).

Egg deposition. Late June to early July. Eggs probably laid in depressions under boulders or in hollow logs. Incubation period of 48 to 49 days in Kansas (Fitch 1970).

Clutch size. 2 to 8 eggs (Wright and Wright 1957:106), typically 5 (McCauley 1945:55).

Eggs hatch. August to September.

Home range/movement. About 0.25 ac (0.1 ha) in Kentucky (Barbour 1971:240). Average for 10 individuals in a forested mountainous area of Kentucky was 253 m² or 0.025 ha (Barbour et al. 1969b).

Food habits/preferences. Earthworms, soft-bodied insects and their larvae, grubs, or slugs.

Comments. Nocturnal and secretive. Fossorial, it has extended periods of inactivity.

Selected references. Schmidt and Davis 1941; Wright and Wright 1957, Barbour, Harvey, and Hardin 1969b.

Northern black racer

Coluber c. constrictor
Squamata, Serpentes
Colubridae

Range. Southern Maine to s.w. Ohio, south to central Alabama to South Carolina and throughout the e. United States.

Relative abundance. Locally abundant.

Habitat. Moist or dry areas, forests and wooded areas, fields, roadsides, swamps, marshes, clearings, near old buildings, trap rock ridges (M. Klemens, pers. commun.), stone walls, and farms. Has been found in deciduous and pine forests. Partially arboreal. Will use ledges for sunning.

Hibernates in large congregations, sometimes with copperheads and rattlesnakes, often using deep rock crevices or abandoned woodchuck holes. Among the earliest snakes to emerge from hibernation.

Age/size at sexual maturity. Males at 13 to 14 months (Fitch 1960b), males 680 to 1,595 mm, females 710 to 1,683 mm (Wright and Wright 1957:135).

Breeding period. May to early June.

Egg deposition. June to early July. Laid in rotting wood, stumps, decaying vegetable matter, loose soil.

Clutch size. 7 to 31 eggs, typically 16 to 17, clutch size proportional to size of female (Fitch 1963:420).

Incubation period. Average of 51 days (Fitch 1970).

Eggs hatch. Late August to September.

Home range/movement. Very territorial; appears to have definite home range (Smith 1956:239). Average distance of 903 ft (275.2 m) in mixed Maryland habitat for 3 individuals after 2 years (Stickel and Cope 1947). Requires large tracts of mixed old fields and woodlands (M. Klemens, pers. commun.).

Food habits/preferences. Varied diet includes small mammals, insects,

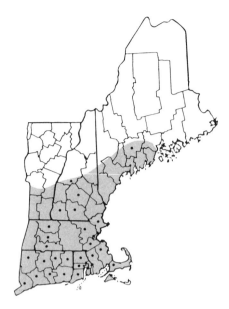

frogs, toads, small birds, birds' eggs, snakes, and lizards (Uhler et al. 1939). Small mammals and insects are 50% of diet (Surface 1906).

Comments. Diurnal.

Selected references. Fitch 1963; Wilson 1978.

Eastern smooth green snake

Opheodrys v. vernalis
Serpentes
Colubridae

Range. Nova Scotia, s. Ontario, into central Minnesota to s. Wisconsin, Michigan, n.e. Ohio to the Appalachians of Virginia and West Virginia and north from central New Jersey throughout New England with the possible exception of n. Maine.

Relative abundance. Common, but currently declining in s. New England, New Jersey, and Michigan.

Habitat. Upland areas, grassy fields, mountain meadows; high altitude areas with grassy, open spots. Also found in open aspen stands, sphagnum bogs, marshes, in vines and brambles, and hardwood stands. Abandoned farmland dominated by successional vegetation and man-made debris on Long Island, New York (Schlauch 1975).

Special habitat requirements. Upland grassy openings.

Age/size at sexual maturity. Probably second year (Seibert and Hagen 1947).

Breeding period. Spring and late summer (Behler and King 1979:640); late August in Ontario (Smith 1956:236).

Egg deposition. Late July to August.

Clutch size. 3 to 12 eggs (Wright and Wright 1957:558), typically 7 (Blanchard 1933a). Oviparous. Nest sites may be used by several females.

Incubation period. Varies from 4 to 23 days (Blanchard 1933a).

Eggs hatch. August to early September.

Home range/movement. Less than 30 yd (27.4 m) for 10 of 12 individuals studied in an uncultivated field in Illinois (Seibert and Hagen 1947).

Food habits/preferences. Insects comprise 73 % of prey items. Also eats spiders and snails (Surface 1906). Salamanders, millipedes, centipedes, particularly caterpillars, orthopterans, ants, flies (Uhler et al. 1939).

Comments. Hibernates early fall to April or May. Population decline may be related to insecticide spraying and loss of open fields and pasture.

Selected references. Schmidt and Davis 1941; Seibert and Hagen 1947; Wright and Wright 1957.

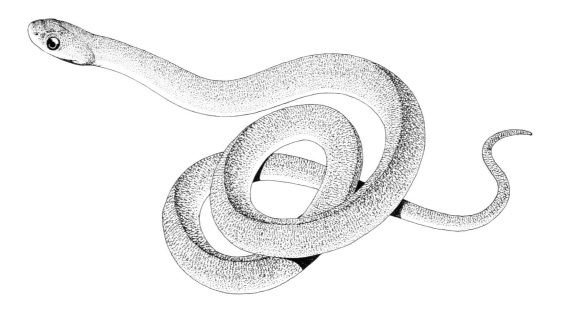

Black rat snake

Elaphe o. obsoleta
Serpentes
Colubridae

Range. Southwestern New England west through s. New York to s. central Illinois, and the Mississippi River area in Wisconsin, south to Oklahoma, central Louisiana, and Georgia. Range may be extending northward in the Connecticut River Valley (T. Tyning, pers. commun.).

Relative abundance. Locally common.
Habitat. Variety of habitats including woodlands, thickets, field edges, farmlands, rocky hillsides and mountaintops, river bottoms, old barns. Readily climbs trees. Found in dry oak and oak-hickory woods, and mesic bottomland forests, may occur in very dense woods (Wright and Wright 1957:232). May reside in cavities in hollow trees (Conant 1975:194). In Connecticut found in gorges and some coastal areas (M. Klemens, pers. commun.).

Hibernates late November to April. May use talus slopes, cisterns, or unused wells. Often found in groups with copperheads and rattlesnakes where these snakes occur.
Age/size at sexual maturity. At 4 years (Fitch 1970). Males 1,095 to 1,835 mm, females 715 to 1,800 mm (Wright and Wright 1957:233).
Breeding period. May to June.
Gestation period. 8 to 12 weeks (Oliver 1955:243).
Egg deposition. July to August. Laid in loose soil, decaying wood, manure piles, sawdust piles.

Clutch size. 6 to 24 eggs, typically 14.
Eggs hatch. Late August to early October.
Home range/movement. Average at least 600 m in diameter for males, and at least 500 m for females in woods and fields in Maryland (Stickel et al. 1980).
Food habits/preferences. Small mammals comprise 60% of prey items, particularly rodents, small birds and their eggs (30%); also amphibians, insects, spiders (Uhler et al. 1939). Young opossums, weasels, owls, and sparrow hawks have been captured as food (Minton 1972:273). Prey is killed by constriction.
Comments. Formerly pilot or pilot black snake. Diurnal and arboreal.
Selected references. Schmidt and Davis 1941; Smith 1956; Wright and Wright 1957; Anderson 1965; Stickel et al. 1980.

Eastern milk snake

Lampropeltis t. triangulum
Serpentes
Colubridae

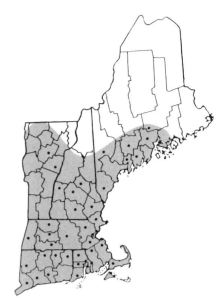

Range. Southeastern Maine and s. Ontario to central Minnesota, south to Tennessee and w. North Carolina and throughout the Northeast. Intergrades with the scarlet king snake (*L. t. elapsoides*) in the southwestern and southeastern portion of its range.
Relative abundance. Common.
Habitat. Various habitats, usually with brushy or woody cover, from sea level to mountain elevations. Usually found under cover. Farmlands, woods, outbuildings, meadows, river bottoms, bogs, rocky hillsides, rodent runways (M. Klemens, pers. commun.). Found under logs, stones, boards, well covers, stones in creek bottoms (M. Stewart, pers. commun.), or other cover during the day. In pine forests, second-growth pine, bog woods, hardwoods, aspen stands. Hibernates from October or November to April.
Special habitat requirements. Suitable cover or loose soil for egg laying.
Age/size at sexual maturity. Third or fourth year (Fitch and Fleet 1970), males to 1,115 mm, females 404 to 966 mm (Wright and Wright 1957:371).
Breeding period. June (Wright and Wright 1957:371).
Egg deposition. Mid-June to July, in piles of soil, sawdust, or manure, or under other cover, often in a communal nest site.
Clutch size. 6 to 24 eggs, typically 13.
Incubation period. 6 to 8 weeks (Wright and Wright 1957:371).
Eggs hatch. Late August to October.
Home range/movement. About 50 ac (20.25 ha) for *L. t. sypspila*, movements of 250 to 1,300 ft (76.2 to 396.2 m) in open woodland in n.e. Kansas (Fitch and Fleet 1970). Seasonal movements probable from dryer hibernation sites to moist bottomlands for the summer (Breckenridge 1958 cited in Williams 1978:79).
Food habits/preferences. Mice, other small mammals, other snakes, lizards, birds and their eggs, slugs.

Mice comprised 72 % of the volume of stomach contents of 42 milk snakes in Pennsylvania (Surface 1908). Forages for food at night.
Comments. Typically nocturnal. Numbers may be declining as abandoned fields revert to forests (T. Tyning, pers. commun.).
Selected references. Schmidt and Davis 1941; Wright and Wright 1957; Fitch and Fleet 1970.

Northern copperhead

Agkistrodon contortrix mokeson
Serpentes
Viperidae

Range. Southwestern New England to s.w. Illinois, south to central Georgia and through central North Carolina.

Relative abundance. Uncommon to rare.

Habitat. Usually associated with deciduous forests. Occupies varied habitats from swamps to mountain tops. Prefers areas with damp leaf litter (Fitch 1960a:116). Exposed mountainous rocky hillsides, talus slopes, basalt ridges, ledges, open woods. Found in habitats with large rocks, rotting wood, and sawdust piles. During summer months may be found near swamps, ponds, or streams. Largely outside of white pine–northern hardwood, and beech-maple associations (Fitch 1960a:123).

Special habitat requirements. Rocky hillsides, talus slopes.

Age/size at sexual maturity. Males during their second summer, females at 3 years (Fitch 1960a:272).

Breeding period. After emergence from hibernation in April to May, peak in late May. Sperm may remain viable in the female for more than a year after copulation (Allen 1955). Gestation period of 105 to 110 days (Fitch 1960a:116).

Young born. August to September, typically September in the Northeast. Viviparous.

No. young. 1 to 17 young, typically 5 to 6 (Wright and Wright 1957:913). Litters produced in alternate years.

Home range/movement. In mixed habitat of woodlands, ledges, and grassland in Kansas. Fitch (1960a:147–49) recorded 24.4 ac (9.7 ha) for males and 8.5 ac (3.4 ha) for females. Seasonal movements occur between hibernaculum and lowland areas.

Food habits/preferences. Mice, other small rodents, insects, small birds, salamanders, lizards, small snakes, frogs, toads. Food obtained by ambush.

Comments. Nocturnal during summer months, diurnal in spring and fall. Has survived eradication in some areas due to cryptic coloration and retiring habits. Usually gregarious. During hibernation (from October to April) sometimes found with other species of snakes including rattlesnakes, but mutually exclusive in Connecticut (Petersen 1970). Den sites are reused each year—a major limiting factor.

Selected references. Schmidt and Davis 1941; Smith 1956; Wright and Wright 1957; Fitch 1960a; Anderson 1965.

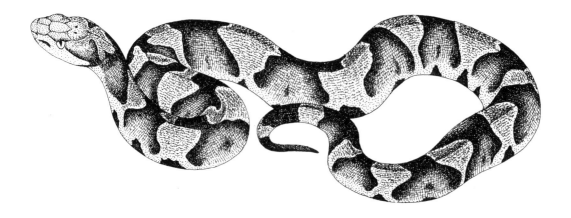

Timber rattlesnake

Crotalus horridus
Serpentes
Viperidae

Range. Southern New Hampshire, the Champlain Valley to s.w. New York, west along the Ohio River Valley and north to the Mississippi River in Wisconsin. Extending to n. Texas, s. Illinois, n. Georgia, and through the Appalachians to New Jersey.

Relative abundance. Uncommon to rare.

Habitat. Timbered areas with rocky outcroppings, dry ridges and second growth deciduous or coniferous forests with high rodent populations. Usually southern exposures. Sometimes in swamps, quarries, old stone walls, abandoned buildings. Often found near streams in late summer. Most common in areas not frequented by man (few such sites remain). Reaches elevations of 6,000 ft (1,800 m) in the Southeast, but probably not found at highest elevations in the Northeast due to harsh climatic conditions (Klauber 1972:511).

Hibernates from September to April in large numbers in rocky crevices usually overgrown with brush. Found with copperheads and other snakes, due to paucity of hibernac-

ula (T. Tyning, pers. commun.).

Special habitat requirements. Rock outcroppings on forested hillsides.

Age/size at sexual maturity. Probably 3½ to 4 years (Klauber 1972:335).

Breeding period. Fall in Connecticut (T. Tyning, pers. commun.) and Wisconsin (Messeling 1953). After emerging from hibernation (Fitch 1970). Gestation period probably about 5½ to 6 months.

Young born. Late August to September, probably biennial cycles (Klauber 1972:691). Viviparous.

No. young. 5 to 17 young, typically 7 to 10 (Klauber 1972:733).

Home range/movement. Females return to hibernation dens to give birth to young. Hibernation dens may be used year after year. Home ranges and favored refuges probably exist, but few investigations have been conducted (Klauber 1972:606–7).

Food habits/preferences. Prefers warm-blooded prey. Small mammals comprise 87% of prey taken (Uhler et al. 1939), particularly mice, but includes rabbits, shrews, chipmunks, squirrels, bats, songbirds, and other snakes. Forages at night (Kimball 1978).

Comments. Extirpated from much of its former range; over-collection and habitat disturbance are serious threats to *Crotalus horridus* in the Northeast. Danger to humans is grossly exaggerated. Vermont was the last New England state to remove a bounty on the timber rattlesnake (1971).

Selected references. Wright and Wright 1957; Anderson 1965; Klauber 1972; Collins and Knight 1980.

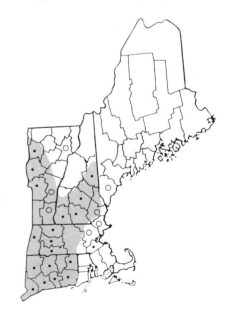

Bibliography

A

Adler, K. K. 1961. Egg-laying in the spotted turtle, *Clemmys gutta* (Schneider). *Ohio J. Sci.* 61:180–82.

Alexander, M. M. 1943. Food habits of the snapping turtle in Connecticut. *J. Wildl. Manage.* 7:278–82.

Allard, H. A. 1935. The natural history of the box turtle. *Sci. Monthly* 41:325–38.

Allen, G. M. 1899. Notes on reptiles and amphibians of Intervale, New Hampshire. *Proc. Boston Soc. Nat. Hist.* 29:63–75.

Allen, J. A. 1868. Catalogue of the reptiles and batrachians found in the vicinity of Springfield, Massachusetts, with notices of all the other species known to inhabit the state. *Proc. Boston Soc. Nat. Hist.* 12:171–204, 248–50.

———. 1870. Notes on Massachusetts reptiles and batrachians. *Proc. Boston Soc. Nat. Hist.* 13:260–63.

Allen, W. B. 1955. Some notes on reptiles. *Herpetologica* 11:228.

Anderson, J. D. 1967a. *Ambystoma maculatum. Cat. Am. Amphib. Rept.* 51.1–51.4.

———. 1967b. *Ambystoma opacum. Cat. Am. Amphib. Rept.* 46.1–46.2.

Anderson, J. D., and R. V. Giacosie. 1967. *Ambystoma laterale* in New Jersey. *Herpetologica* 23:108–11.

Anderson, P. 1965. *The reptiles of Missouri.* Columbia: Univ. Missouri Press.

Ashton, R. E., Jr. 1975. A study of movement, home range, and winter behavior of *Desmognathus fuscus* (Rafinesque). *J. Herpetol.* 9:85–91.

———. 1976. *Endangered and threatened amphibians and reptiles in the United States.* Soc. Study Amphib. Rept., Misc. Publ., Herpetol. Circ. 5.

Ashton, R. E., and P. S. Ashton. 1978. Movements and winter behavior of *Eurycea bislineata* (Amphibia, Urodela, Plethodontidae). *J. Herpetol.* 12:295–98.

Austin, N. E., and J. P. Bogart. 1982. Erythrocyte area and ploidy determination in the salamanders of the *Ambystoma jeffersonianum* complex. *Copeia* 1982 (2): 485–88.

B

Babbitt, L. H. 1937. The amphibia of Connecticut. Hartford: State Geol. and Nat. Hist. Surv. Bull. no. 57:9–50.

Babcock, H. L. 1919. The turtles of New England. *Memoirs of the Boston Soc. of Nat. Hist.* 8:325–431. Reprinted 1971: *Turtles of the northeastern United States.* New York: Dover Publication.

———. 1921. Some interesting New England reptiles. *Bull. Boston Soc. Nat. Hist.* 26:4–8.

———. 1925. Rattlesnakes in Massachusetts. *Bull. Boston Soc. Nat. Hist.* 35:5–10.

———. 1926. The copperhead. *Bull. Boston Soc. Nat. Hist.* 41:3–6.

———. 1929. *Snakes of New England.* Boston: Soc. Nat. Hist., Nat. Hist. Guide no. 1.

Bailey, R. M. 1949. Temperature tolerance of garter snakes in hibernation. *Ecology* 30:238–42.

Ball, S. C. 1933. The spadefoot toad in Connecticut in 1933. Pp. 26–30. In Babbitt 1937.

———. 1936. The distribution and behavior of the spadefoot toad in Connecticut. *Trans. Connecticut Acad. Arts and Sci.* 32:351–79.

Banasiak, C. F. 1974. Population structure and reproductive ecology of the red-backed salamander in DDT-treated forests of northern Maine. Ph.D. diss., Univ. Maine, Orono.

Barbour, R. W. 1971. *Amphibians and reptiles of Kentucky.* Lexington: Univ. Press of Kentucky.

Barbour, R. W., J. W. Hardin, J. P. Schafer, and M. J. Harvey. 1969a. Home range, movement, and activity of the dusky salamander, *Desmognathus fuscus. Copeia* 1969(2):293–97.

Barbour, R. W., M. J. Harvey, and J. W. Hardin. 1969b. Home range, movement, and activity of the eastern worm snake, *Carphophis a. amoenus. Ecology* 50:470–76.

Barrett, J. W. 1962. *Regional silviculture of the United States.* New York: Ronald Press.

Barthalmus, G. T., and E. D. Bellis. 1969. Homing in the northern dusky salamander, *Desmognathus f. fuscus* (Rafinesque). *Copeia* 1969(1):148–53.

Barton, A. J. 1957. Our knowledge of the bog turtle, *Clemmys muhlenbergi,* further augmented. M.S. thesis, Univ. Pittsburgh.

Barton, A. J., and J. W. Price. 1955. Our knowledge of the bog turtle, *Clemmys muhlenbergi,* surveyed and augmented. *Copeia* 1955(3):159–65.

Behler, J. L., and F. W. King. 1979. *The Audubon Society field guide to North American reptiles and amphibians.* New York: Alfred A. Knopf, Inc.

Bellis, E. D. 1961. Growth of the wood frog, *Rana sylvatica. Copeia* 1961(1):74–77.

———. 1965. Home range and movements of the wood frog in a northern bog. *Ecology* 46:90–98.

———. 1968. Summer movement of red-spotted newts in a small pond. *J. Herpetol.* 1:86–91.

Bishop, S. C. 1941. The salamanders of New York. *New York State Mus. Bull.* 324: 1–365.

———. 1947. *Handbook of salamanders. The salamanders of the United States, of Canada, and Lower California.* Ithaca, N.Y.: Comstock.

Blanchard, F. N. 1923. The life history of the four-toed salamander. *Am. Nat.* 57: 262–68.

———. 1930. Further studies on the eggs and young of the eastern ringneck snake, *Diadophis punctatus edwardsii. Bull. Antivenin Inst. Am.* 4:4–10. (Information obtained from Wright and Wright 1957.)

———. 1933a. Eggs and young of the smooth green snake, *Liopeltis vernalis* (Harlan). *Pap. Mich. Acad. Sci.* 17: 493–508.

———. 1933b. Late autumn collections and hibernating situations of the salamander, *Hemidactylium scutatum* (Schlegel), in southern Michigan. *Copeia* 1933 (4):216–17.

———. 1934. The relation of the four-toed salamander to her nest. *Copeia* 1934(3):137–38.

———. 1937a. Data on the natural history of the red-bellied snake, *Storeria occipito-maculata* (Storer), in northern Michigan. *Copeia* 1937(3):151–62.

———. 1937b. Eggs and natural nests of the eastern ring-neck snake, *Diadophis punctatus edwardsii. Pap. Mich. Acad. Sci.* 22:521–32.

Blanchard, F. N., and F. C. Blanchard. 1942. Mating of the garter snake, *Thamnophis s. sirtalis* (Linnaeus). *Pap. Mich. Acad. Sci.* 27:215–34.

Bleakney, J. S. 1952. The amphibians and reptiles of Nova Scotia. *Can. Field-Nat.* 66:125–29.

———. 1957. The egg-laying habits of the salamander, *Ambystoma jeffersonianum. Copeia* 1957(2):141–42.

———. 1958. A zoogeographical study of the amphibians and reptiles of eastern Canada. *Nat. Mus. of Canada Bull.* no. 155, Biol. series no. 54.

———. 1959. *Thamnophis s. sirtalis* (Linnaeus) in eastern Canada, redescription of *T. s. pallidula* (Allen). *Copeia* 1959(1): 52–56.

Blem, C. R. 1981. *Heterodon platyrhinos* Latreille. *Cat. Am. Amphib. Rept.* 282. 1–282.2.

Bragg, A. N. 1956. *Gnomes of the night, the spadefoot toads.* Philadelphia: Univ. Penn. Press.

Brandon, R. A. 1961. A comparison of the larvae of five northeastern species of *Ambystoma* (Amphibia, Caudata). *Copeia* 1961(4):377–83.

———. 1967. *Gyrinophilus porphyriticus* (Green). *Cat. Am. Amphib. Rept.* 33.1–33.3.

Breckenridge, W. J. 1958. *Reptiles and amphibians of Minnesota.* 2d ed. Minneapolis: Univ. Minn. Press.

Breder, R. B. 1927. Turtle trailing: a new technique for studying the life habits of certain testudinata. *Zoologica* 9:231–43.

Brodie, E. D. 1968. Investigations on the skin toxin of the red-spotted newt, *Notophthalmus v. viridescens. Am. Midl. Nat.* 80:276–80.

Brown, E. E. 1979. Stray food records from New York and Michigan snakes. *Am. Midl. Nat.* 102:200–203.

Bruce, R. C. 1969. Fecundity in primitive plethodontid salamanders. *Evolution* 23: 50–54.

———. 1972. Variation in the life cycle of the salamander *Gyrinophilus porphyriticus. Herpetologica* 28:230–45.

———. 1980. A model of the larval period of the spring salamander, *Gyrinophilus porphyriticus*, based on size-frequency distributions. *Herpetologica* 36: 78–86.

Bumpus, H. C. 1885. Reptiles and amphibians of Rhode Island. V. *Random Notes Nat. Hist.* 2:13.

Burger, J. W. 1935. *Plethodon cinereus*

(Green) in eastern Pennsylvania and New Jersey. *Am. Nat.* 69:578–86.

Burton, T. M. 1976. An analysis of the feeding ecology of the salamanders (Amphibia, Urodela) of the Hubbard Brook Experimental Forest, New Hampshire. *J. Herpetol.* 10:187–204.

———. 1977. Population estimates, feeding habits and nutrient and energy relationships of *Notophthalmus v. viridescens*, in Mirror Lake, New Hampshire. *Copeia* 1977(1):139–43.

Burton, T. M., and G. E. Likens. 1975. Salamander populations and biomass in Hubbard Brook Experimental Forest, New Hampshire. *Copeia* 1975(3):541–46.

Bury, R. B. 1979. Review of the ecology and conservation of the bog turtle, *Clemmys muhlenbergii.* U.S. Fish and Wildl. Serv. Spec. Sci. Rep., Wildl. No. 219.

C

Cagle, F. R. 1942. Herpetological fauna of Jackson and Union Counties, Illinois. *Am. Midl. Nat.* 28:164–200. (Information obtained from Smith 1961.)

———. 1944. Home range, homing behavior, and migration in turtles. *Misc. Publ. Mus. Zool., Univ. Mich.* No. 61: 1–34.

———. 1950. The life history of the slider turtle, *Pseudemys scripta troostii* (Holbrook). *Ecol. Monogr.* 20:31–54.

Cahn, A. R. 1937. The turtles of Illinois. *Illinois Biol. Monogr.* 16:1–218. (Information obtained from Conant 1938.)

Caldwell, R. S. 1975. Observations on the winter activity of the red-backed salamander, *Plethodon cinereus,* in Indiana. *Herpetologica* 31:21–22.

Carpenter, C. C. 1952a. Growth and maturity of three species of *Thamnophis* in Michigan. *Copeia* 1952(4):237–43.

———. 1952b. Comparative ecology of the common garter snake (*Thamnophis s. sirtalis*), the ribbon snake (*Thamnophis s. sauritus*), and Butler's garter snake (*Thamnophis butleri*) in mixed populations. *Ecol. Monogr.* 22:235–58.

Carr, A. F. 1952. *Handbook of turtles of the United States, Canada, and Baja California.* Ithaca, N.Y.: Comstock.

Center for Natural Areas. 1976. Reptiles and amphibians. Pp. 260–65. In *A preliminary listing of noteworthy and natural features in Maine.* Augusta, Me.: State Planning Office.

Clarke, R. D. 1974. Activity and movement patterns in a population of Fowler's toad, *Bufo woodhousii fowleri. Am. Midl. Nat.* 92:257–74.

Collins, J. T., R. Conant, J. E. Huheey, J. L. Knight, E. M. Rundquist, and H. M. Smith. 1982. *Standard common and current scientific names for North American amphibians and reptiles.* 2d ed. Herpetological circular no. 12. Publ. by Soc. for the Study of Amph. and Reptiles.

Collins, J. T., and J. L. Knight. 1980. *Crotalus horridus.* Linnaeus. *Cat. Am. Amphib. Rept.* 253.1–253.2.

Conant, R. 1957. *Reptiles and amphibians of the Northeastern states.* 3d ed. Philadelphia: Zool. Soc. of Philadelphia.

———. 1975. *A field guide to reptiles and amphibians of eastern and central North America.* 2d ed. Boston: Houghton Mifflin Co.

Cooper, J. E. 1956. Aquatic hibernation of the red-backed salamander. *Herpetologica* 12:165–66.

———. 1959. The turtle *Pseudemys scripta feral* in Maryland. *Herpetologica* 15:44.

Craig, R. J. 1979. *The rare vertebrates of Connecticut.* USDA Soil Conservation Service, Storrs, Ct.

Currie, W., and E. D. Bellis. 1969. Home range and movements of the bullfrog, *Rana catesbeiana* (Shaw), in an Ontario Pond. *Copeia* 1969(4):688–92.

D

Danstedt, R. T., Jr. 1975. Local geographic variation in demographic parameters and body size of *Desmognathus fuscus* (Amphibia, Plethodontidae). *Ecology* 56:1054–67.

Davidson, J. A. 1956. Notes on the food habits of the slimy salamander, *Plethodon g. glutinosus. Herpetologica* 12:129–31.

Delzell, D. E. 1958. Spatial movement and growth of *Hyla crucifer.* Ph.D. diss., Univ. Mich. [From Diss. Abstr. 19(6): 1478, 1958.]

Dickerson, M. C. 1969. *The frog book.* New York: Dover Publ., Inc. (Originally printed 1906. Doubleday, Page and Co.)

Dole, J. W. 1965. Summer movements of adult leopard frogs, *Rana pipiens* (Schreber), in northern Michigan. *Ecology* 46: 236–55.

———. 1968. Homing in leopard frogs, *Rana pipiens. Ecology* 49:386–99.

Douglas, M. E., and B. L. Monroe. 1981. A comparative study of topographical orientation in *Ambystoma* (Amphibia: Caudata). *Copeia* 1981(2):460–63.

Drake, C. J. 1914. The food of *Rana pipiens* (Schreber). *Ohio Nat.* 14:257–69.

Driver, E. C. 1936. Observations on *Scaphiopus holbrooki* (Harlan). *Copeia* 1936(1): 67–69.

Drowne, F. P. 1905. The reptiles and batrachians of Rhode Island. *Roger Williams Park Mus. Monograph* 15:1–24.

Dunn, E. R. 1926. *The salamanders of the family Plethodontidae.* Northampton, Mass.: Smith College. 50th Anniv. Publ.

E

Edgren, R. A. 1955. The natural history of the hog-nosed snakes, genus *Heterodon:* a review. *Herpetologica* 11:105–17.

———. 1960. Ovulation time in the musk turtle, *Sternotherus odoratus* (Latreille). *Nat. Hist. Misc.* 152:1–3.

Elick, G. E., J. A. Sealander, and R. J. Beumer. 1979. Temperature preferenda, body temperature tolerances, and habitat selection of small Colubrid snakes. *Trans. Missouri Acad. Sci.* 13:21–31.

Emlen, S. T. 1968. Territoriality in the bullfrog, *Rana catesbeiana. Copeia* 1968(2): 240–43.

Ernst, C. H. 1968a. Homing ability in the spotted turtle, *Clemmys guttata* (Schneider). *Herpetologica* 24:77–78.

———. 1968b. A turtle's territory. *Int. Turtle and Tortoise Soc. J.* 2(6):9, 34.

———. 1970. Home range of the spotted turtle. *Copeia* 1970(2):391–92.

———. 1971. *Chrysemys picta* (Schneider). *Cat. Am. Amphib. Rept.* 106.1–106.4.

———. 1972a. *Clemmys guttata* (Schneider). *Cat. Am. Amphib. Rept.* 124.1–124.2.

———. 1972b. *Clemmys insculpta* (LeConte). *Cat. Am. Amphib. Rept.* 125.1–125.2.

———. 1977. Biological notes on the bog turtle, *Clemmys muhlenbergii. Herpetologica* 33:241–46.

Ernst, C. H., and R. W. Barbour. 1972. *Turtles of the United States.* Lexington: Univ. Press of Kentucky.

Ernst, C. H., and R. B. Bury. 1977. *Clemmys muhlenbergii* (Schoepff). *Cat. Am. Amphib. Rept.* 204.1–204.2.

Ewing, H. E. 1943. Continued fertility in the female box turtles following mating.

Copeia 1943(2):112–14.

F

Farrell, R. F., and R. T. Zappalorti. 1979. The ecology and distribution of the wood turtle, *Clemmys insculpta* (LeConte), New Jersey, Pt. 1. [Preliminary report on a research contract between the New Jersey Dept. of Environ. Protection, Endangered and Nongame Species Proj., Nat. Audubon Soc. and Herpetological Associates No. 79.03.] Unpublished.

———. 1980. An ecological study of the wood turtle, *Clemmys insculpta* (LeConte), (Reptilia, Testudines, Emydidae) in northern New Jersey, Pt. 2. [Report to the New Jersey Dept. of Environ. Protection, Endangered and Nongame Species Proj., Herpetological Associates Rep. No. 80.02.] Unpublished.

Finneran, L. C. 1948. Reptiles in Branford, Connecticut. *Herpetologica* 4: 123–26.

Fitch, H. S. 1954. Life history and ecology of the five-lined skink, *Eumeces fasciatus. Univ. Kansas Publ., Mus. Nat. Hist.* 8:1–156. (Information obtained from Minton 1972.)

———. 1960a. Autecology of the copperhead. *Univ. Kansas Publ., Mus. Nat. Hist.* 13:185–288.

———. 1960b. Criteria for determining sex and breeding maturity in snakes. *Herpetologica* 16:49–51.

———. 1963. Natural history of the racer *Coluber constrictor. Univ. Kansas Publ., Mus. Nat. Hist.* 15:351–468.

———. 1965. An ecological study of the garter snake, *Thamnophis sirtalis. Univ. Kansas Publ., Mus. Nat. Hist.* 15:493–564.

———. 1970. Reproductive cycles in lizards and snakes. Kansas. Univ. Mus. Nat. Hist., Misc. Publ. no. 52.

———. 1980. *Thamnophis sirtalis* (Linnaeus). *Cat. Am. Amphib. Rept.* 270.1–270.4.

Fitch, H. S., and R. R. Fleet. 1970. Natural history of the milk snake *(Lampropeltis triangulum)* in northeastern Kansas. *Herpetologica* 26:387–96.

Fitzpatrick, L. C. 1973. Energy allocation in the Allegheny Mountain salamander, *Desmognathus ochrophaeus. Ecol. Monogr.* 43:43–58.

Fogg, B. F. 1862. List of reptiles and amphibians found in the state of Maine. *Proc. Portland Soc. of Nat. Hist.* 1:86.

Force, E. R. 1933. The age of attainment of sexual maturity of the leopard frog, *Rana pipiens* (Schreber), in northern Michigan. *Copeia* 1933(3):128–31.

Forester, D. C. 1977. Comments on the female reproductive cycle and philopatry by *Desmognathus ochrophaeus* (Amphibia, Urodela, Plethodontidae). *J. Herpetol.* 11:311–16.

———. 1979. Homing to the nest by female mountain dusky salamander, *Desmognathus ochrophaeus,* with comments on the sensory modalities essential to clutch recognition. *Herpetologica* 35: 330–35.

Fowler, J. A., and R. Sutcliffe. 1952. An additional record for the purple salamander, *Gyrinophilus p. porphyriticus,* from Maine. *Copeia* 1952(1):48–49.

Fraker, M. A. 1970. Home range and homing in the watersnake, *Natrix s. sipedon. Copeia* 1970(4):665–73.

G

Gans, C. 1945. Occurrence of the dusky salamander on Manhattan. *Copeia* 1945(2):118.

Gatz, A. J., Jr. 1971. Critical thermal maxima of *Ambystoma maculatum* and *A. jeffersonianum* in relation to time of breeding. *Herpetologica* 27:157–60.

Gibbons, J. W. 1968a. Reproductive potential, activity and cycles in the painted turtle, *Chrysemys picta. Ecology* 49: 399–409.

———. 1968b. Observations on the ecology and population dynamics of the Blanding's turtle, *Emydoidea blandingi. Can. J. Zool.* 46:288–90.

Gochfeld, M. 1975. The decline of the eastern garter snake, *Thamnophis s. sirtalis,* in a rural residential section of Westchester County, New York. *Engelhardtia* 6(3):23–24.

Gordon, D. M. 1980. An investigation of the ecology of the map turtle, *Graptemys geographica* (LeSueur), in the northern part of its range. *Can. J. Zool.* 58:2210–30.

Gordon, R. E. 1968. Terrestrial activity of the spotted salamander, *Ambystoma maculatum. Copeia* 1968(4):879–80.

Gosner, K., and J. H. Black. 1955. The effects of temperature and moisture on the reproductive cycle of *Scaphiopus h. holbrooki. Am. Midl. Nat.* 54:192–203.

Graham, T. E. 1971a. Growth rate of the red-bellied turtle, *Chrysemys rubriventris,* at Plymouth, Massachusetts. *Copeia* 1971(2):353–56.

———. 1971b. Eggs and hatchlings of the red-bellied turtle, *Chrysemys rubriventris*, from Plymouth, Massachusetts. *J. Herpetol.* 5:59–60.

———. 1980. Red-belly blues. *Animals* 113:17–21.

———. 1982. Second find of *Pseudemys rubriventris* at Ipswich, Massachusetts, and refutation of the Naushon Island record. *Herpetol. Rev.* 13(3):82–83.

Graham, T. E., and T. S. Doyle. 1977. Growth and population characteristics of Blanding's turtle, *Emydoidea blandingii*, in Massachusetts. *Herpetologica* 33: 410–14.

———. 1979. Dimorphism, courtship, eggs, and hatchlings of the Blanding's turtle, *Emydoidea blandingii* (Reptilia, Testudines, Emydidae), in Massachusetts. *J. Herpetol.* 13:125–27.

Graham, T. E., and V. H. Hutchinson. 1969. Centenarian box turtles. *Int. Turtle and Tortoise Soc. J.* 3(3):24–29.

———. 1979. Effect of temperature and photoperiod acclimatization on thermal preferences of selected freshwater turtles. *Copeia* 1979(1):165–69.

Grant, W. C. 1955. Territorialism in two species of salamanders. *Science* 121: 137–38.

Grizzell, R. A., Jr. 1949. The hibernation site of three snakes and a salamander. *Copeia* 1949(3):231–32.

Groves, J. D. 1982. Egg-eating behavior of brooding five-lined skinks, *Eumeces fasciatus*. *Copeia* 1982(4):969–71.

H

Hairston, N. H. 1949. The local distribution and ecology of the plethodontid salamanders of the southern Appalachians. *Ecol. Monogr.* 19:47–73.

Hamilton, W. J., Jr. 1932. The food and feeding habits of some eastern salamanders. *Copeia* 1932(1):83–86.

———. 1934. The rate of growth of the toad [*Bufo a. americanus* (Holbrook)] under natural conditions. *Copeia* 1934(2): 88–90.

———. 1948. The food and feeding behavior of the green frog, *Rana clamitans* (Latreille), in New York state. *Copeia* 1948(3):203–7.

———. 1951. The food and feeding behavior of the garter snake in New York.

Am. Midl. Nat. 46:385–90.

———. 1954. The economic status of the toad. *Herpetologica* 10:37–40.

Hammer, D. A. 1969. Parameters of a marsh snapping turtle population, Lacreek Refuge, South Dakota, *J. Wildl. Manage.* 33:995–1005.

Harris, R. N. 1981. Intrapond homing behavior in *Notophthalmus viridescens*. *J. Herpetol.* 15:355–56.

Hassinger, D. D., J. D. Anderson, and G. H. Dalrymple. 1970. The early life history and ecology of *Ambystoma tigrinum* and *Ambystoma opacum* in New Jersey. *Am. Midl. Nat.* 84:474–95.

Healy, W. R. 1974. Population consequences of alternative life histories in *Notophthalmus v. viridescens*. *Copeia* 1974(1):221–29.

Heatwole, H. 1961. Habitat selection and activity of the wood frog, *Rana sylvatica* (LeConte). *Am. Midl. Nat.* 66:301–13.

———. 1962. Environmental factors influencing local distribution and activity of the salamander, *Plethodon cinereus*. *Ecology* 43:460–72.

Hedeen, S. E. 1970. The ecology and life history of the mink frog, *Rana septentrionalis* (Baird). Ph.D. diss., Univ. Minn., Minneapolis. [From Diss. Abstr. 31: 3985B, 1970.]

———. 1972. Postmetamorphic growth and reproduction of the mink frog, *Rana septentrionalis* (Baird). *Copeia* 1972(1): 169–75.

———. 1977. *Rana septentrionalis* (Baird). *Cat. Am. Amphib. Rept.* 202.1–202.2.

Henshaw, J. 1904. List of the Reptilia Fauna of New England. *Occ. Pap. Boston Soc. Nat. Hist.* 7(1):1–13.

Herreid, C. F., and S. Kinney. 1967. Temperature and development of the wood frog, *Rana sylvatica*, in Alaska. *Ecology* 48:579–89.

Highton, R. 1956. The life history of the slimy salamander, *Plethodon glutinosus*, in Florida. *Copeia* 1956(2):75–93.

———. 1962. Geographic variation in the life history of the slimy salamander. *Copeia* 1962(3):597–613.

Hinckley, M. H. 1882. Notes on the development of *Rana sylvatica* LeConte. *Proc. Boston Soc. Nat. Hist.* 22:85–95.

———. 1883. Notes on the peeping frog, *Hyla pickeringii* Le Conte. *Memoirs Boston Soc. Nat. Hist.* 3:311–18.

Hitchcock, E. 1835. *Report on the geology, mineralogy, botany, and zoology of Massachusetts.* Amherst, Mass.: Press of J. S. and C. Adams.

Hoff, J. G. 1977. A Massachusetts hibernation site of the red-backed salamander, *Plethodon cinereus*. *Herpetol. Rev.* 8(2):33.

Hoopes, I. 1930. *Bufo* in New England. *Bull. Boston Soc. Nat. Hist.* 57:13–20.

———. 1938. Marbled salamanders from New Hampshire. *Bull. New England Mus. Nat. Hist.* 87:16–17.

Huheey, J. E., and R. A. Brandon. 1973. Rock-face populations of the mountain salamander, *Desmognathus ochrophaeus*, in North Carolina. *Ecol. Monogr.* 43: 59–77.

Hurlbert, S. H. 1969. The breeding migrations and interhabitat wandering of the vermilion-spotted newt, *Notophthalmus viridescens* (Rafinesque). *Ecol. Monogr.* 39:465–88.

———. 1970. The post-larval migration of the red-spotted newt, *Notophthalmus viridescens* (Rafinesque). *Copeia* 1970(3): 515–28.

Husting, E. L. 1965. Survival and breeding structure in a population of *Ambystoma maculatum*. *Copeia* 1965(3):352–62.

I

Ingram, W. M., and E. C. Raney. 1943. Additional studies on the movement of tagged bullfrogs, *Rana catesbeiana* (Shaw). *Am. Midl. Nat.* 29:239–41.

J

Jameson, E. W., Jr. 1944. Food of the red-backed salamander. *Copeia* 1944(3): 145–47.

Johnson, J. E., and A. S. Goldberg. 1975. Movement of larval two-lined salamanders (*Eurycea bislineata*) in the Mill River, Massachusetts. *Copeia* 1975(3):588–89.

Josselyn, J. 1672. *New England's Rarities.* London: G. Widdowes. Reprint ed. 1865, Boston: William Veazie.

———. 1675. *An account of two voyages to New-England, made during the years 1638, 1663.* London: G. Widdowes. Reprint ed. 1833. Coll. Massachusetts Hist. Soc. 3, 3d ser.

K

Karns, D. R. 1980. Ecological risks for amphibians at toxic bog water breeding sites in northern Minnesota. (Abstract). Proc. 1980 Joint Annu. Herpetologists League/

Soc. for the Study of Amphib. and Reptiles, Milwaukee, Wisconsin.

Keen, W. H. 1979. Feeding and activity patterns in the salamander *Desmognathus ochrophaeus* (Amphibia, Urodela, Plethodontidae). *J. Herpetol.* 13:461–67.

Keen, W. H., and L. P. Orr. 1980. Reproductive cycle, growth and maturation of northern female *Desmognathus ochrophaeus*. *J. Herpetol.* 14:7–10.

Kieran, J. 1959. *A natural history of New York City.* Boston: Houghton Mifflin Co.

Kimball, D., ed. 1978. *The timber rattlesnake in New England.* A symposium. Springfield, Mass.: West. Mass. Herpetol. Soc.

Kiviat, E. 1980. A Hudson River tidemarsh snapping turtle population. Pp. 158–68. In *Trans. Northeast. Sec. Wildl. Soc. 37th Northeast. Fish and Wildl. Conf.,* April 27–30, 1980. Ellenville, N. Y.

Klauber, L. M. 1972. *Rattlesnakes.* 2 vols. Berkeley and Los Angeles: Univ. Calif. Press.

Kleeberger, S. R., and J. K. Werner. 1982. Home range and homing behavior of *Plethodon cinereus* in northern Michigan. *Copeia* 1982(2):409–15.

Kramek, W. C. 1972. Food of the frog *Rana septentrionalis* in New York. *Copeia* 1972(2):390–92.

———. 1976. Feeding behavior of *Rana septentrionalis* (Amphibia, Anura, Ranidae). *J. Herpetol.* 10:251–52.

Krysik, A. J. 1980. Microhabitat selection and brooding phenology of *Desmognathus f. fuscus* in western Pennsylvania. *J. Herpetol.* 14:291–92.

Küchler, A. W. 1964. *Potential natural vegetation of the coterminous United States.* Amer. Geographical Soc. Spec. Pub. no. 36.

L

Lagler, K. F. 1943. Food habits and economic relations of the turtles of Michigan with special reference to game management. *Am. Midl. Nat.* 29:257–312.

Lamson, G. H. 1935. The reptiles of Connecticut. Conn. Geol. Nat. Hist. Surv. Bull. 54.

Landre, E. 1980. The blue-spotted salamander. *Sanctuary.* Bull. Mass. Audubon Soc. 20(4):6–7.

Lazell, J. D., Jr. 1968. Blue-spotted salamander. *Mass. Audubon Soc. Bull.* 53(2):20–25.

———. 1972. *Reptiles and amphibians in Massachusetts.* Lincoln, Mass.: Audubon Soc.

———. 1976a. *This broken archipelago.* New York: Demeter Press, Quadrangle, New York Times Book Co.

———. 1976b. Geographic distribution: *Desmognathus ochrophaeus.* SSAR Herp. Review 7:122.

———. 1979. Teetering toward oblivion. *Mass. Wildl.* 30(4):15–18.

Linsley, J. H. 1843. A catalogue of the reptiles of Connecticut, arranged according to their natural families. *Amer. Journ. Sci. Arts* 46:37–51.

Linzey, D. W. 1967. Food of the leopard frog, *Rana p. pipiens,* in central New York. *Herpetologica* 23:11–17.

Logier, E. B. S. 1952. The frogs, toads and salamanders of eastern Canada. Toronto: Univ. of Toronto Press.

Lotter, F. 1978. Reproductive ecology of the salamander *Plethodon cinereus* (Amphibia, Urodela, Plethodontidae) in Connecticut. *J. Herpetol.* 12:231–36.

Lucas, F. A. 1916. Occurrence of *Pseudemys* at Plymouth, Mass. *Copeia* 38:98–100.

Lynn, W. G., and T. vonBrand. 1945. Studies on the oxygen consumption and water metabolism of turtle embryos. *Biol. Bull.* 88:112–25.

M

MacCoy, C. V. 1930. Records of the pilot black snake in New England. *Bull. Boston Soc. Nat. Hist.* 57:21–22.

———. 1931. Key for identification of New England amph. and reptiles. *Bull. Boston Soc. Nat. Hist.* 59:25–33.

MacNamara, M. C. 1977. Food habits of terrestrial adult migrants and immature red efts of the red-spotted newt, *Notophthalmus viridescens. Herpetologica* 33:127–32.

Mahmoud, I. Y. 1968. Feeding behavior in Kinosternid turtles. *Herpetologica* 24:300–305.

———. 1969. Comparative ecology of the Kinosternid turtles of Oklahoma. *Southwest Nat.* 14:31–66.

Marshall, W. H., and M. F. Buell. 1955. A study of the occurrence of amphibians in relation to a bog succession, Itasca State Park, Minnesota. *Ecology* 36:381–87.

Martof, B. S. 1953a. Territoriality in the green frog, *Rana clamitans. Ecology* 34:165–74.

———. 1953b. Home range and movements of the green frog, *Rana clamitans. Ecology* 34:529–43.

———. 1956. Factors influencing size and composition of populations of *Rana clamitans. Am. Midl. Nat.* 56:224–45.

———. 1970. *Rana sylvatica* (LeConte). *Cat. Am. Amphib. Rept.* 86.1–86.4.

Martof, B. S., W. M. Palmer, J. R. Bailey, and J. R. Harrison, III. 1980. *Amphibians and reptiles of the Carolinas and Virginia.* Chapel Hill, N.C.: Univ. North Carolina Press.

Massachusetts Division of Fisheries and Wildlife. 1978. *Species for special consideration in Massachusetts.* Publ. no. 11094–5–100–12–78–CR.

Masterson, J. R. 1938. Colonial rattlesnake lore, 1714. *Zoologica* 23:213–16.

Maynard, E. A. 1934. The aquatic migration of the toad, *Bufo americanus* (LeConte). *Copeia* 1934(4):174–77.

McCauley, R. H., Jr. 1945. *The reptiles of Maryland and District of Columbia.* Hagerstown, Md.: Publ. by author.

McCoy, C. J. 1973. *Emydoidea blandingii. Cat. Am. Amphib. Rept.* 136.1–136.4.

McCoy, C. J., and A. V. Bianculli. 1966. The distribution and dispersal of *Heterodon platyrhinos* in Pennsylvania. *J. Ohio Herpetol. Soc.* 5(4):153–58.

McFarland, W. N., F. H. Pough, T. J. Cade, and J. B. Heiser. 1979. *Vertebrate life.* New York: Macmillan.

Mecham, J. S. 1967. *Notophthalmus viridescens. Cat. Am. Amphib. Rept.* 53.1–53.4.

Messeling, E. 1953. Rattlesnakes in southwestern Wisconsin. *Wis. Conserv. Bull.* No. 18(10):21–23.

Minton, S. A., Jr. 1944. Introduction to the study of the reptiles of Indiana. *Am. Midl. Nat.* 32:438–77.

———. 1954. Salamanders of the *Ambystoma jeffersonianum* complex in Indiana. *Herpetologica* 10:173–79.

———. 1972. *Amphibians and reptiles of Indiana.* Indianapolis: Indiana Acad. Sci.

Mittleman, M. B. 1966. *Eurycea bislineata* (Green). *Cat. Am. Amphib. Rept.* 45.1–45.4.

Moore, J. E., and E. H. Strickland. 1955.

Further notes on the food of Alberta amphibians. *Am. Midl. Nat.* 54:253–56.

Morgan, A. H., and M. C. Grierson. 1932. Winter habits and yearly food consumption of adult spotted newts, *Triturus viridescens. Ecology* 13:54–62.

N

Neill, W. T. 1963. *Hemidactylium scutatum. Cat. Am. Amphib. Rept.* 2.1–2.2.

Nemuras, K. 1969. Survival of the Muhlenberg. *Int. Turtle and Tortoise Soc. J.* 3(5):18–21.

Newman, H. H. 1906. The habits of certain tortoises. *J. Comp. Neur. Psych.* 16:126–52.

Nichols, J. T. 1939. Range and homing of individual box turtles. *Copeia* 1939(3):125–27.

Noble, G. K., and M. K. Brady. 1933. Observations on the life history of the marbled salamander, *Ambystoma opacum* (Gravenhorst). *Zoologica* 11:89–132.

Noble, G. K., and H. J. Clausen. 1936. The aggregation behavior of *Storeria dekayi* and other snakes, with especial reference to the sense organs involved. *Ecol. Monogr.* 6:269–316.

O

Obbard, M. E., and R. J. Brooks. 1980. Nesting migrations of the snapping turtle (*Chelydra serpentina*). *Herpetologica* 36:158–62.

Oldham, R. S. 1966. Spring movements in the American toad, *Bufo americanus. Can. J. Zool.* 44:63–100.

Oliver, J. A. 1955. *The natural history of North American amphibians and reptiles.* Princeton, N.J.: D. Van Nostrand Co., Inc.

Oliver, J. A., and J. R. Bailey. 1939. Amphibians and reptiles of New Hampshire. Pp. 195–217. In *Biol. Surv. Conn. Watershed* rept. no. 4.

Oplinger, C. S. 1967. Food habits and feeding activity of recently transformed and adult *Hyla c. crucifer* (Wied). *Herpetologica* 23:209–17.

Organ, J. A. 1961. Studies of the local distribution, life history, and population dynamics of the salamander genus *Desmognathus* in Virginia. *Ecol. Monogr.* 31:189–220.

P

Palmer, E. L. 1949. *Fieldbook of natural history.* New York: McGraw-Hill.

Pearse, A. S. 1923. The abundance and migration of turtles. *Ecology* 4:24–28.

Pearson, P. G. 1955. Population ecology of the spadefoot toad, *Scaphiopus h. holbrooki. Ecol. Monogr.* 25:233–67.

———. 1957. Further notes on the population ecology of the spadefoot toad. *Ecology* 38:580–86.

Petersen, R. C. 1970. *Connecticut's venomous snakes.* Hartford, Conn.: State Geol. and Nat. Hist. Surv. Bull. No. 103.

Pope, C. H. 1939. Turtles of the United States and Canada. New York: Alfred A. Knopf, Inc. Reprint 1946.

———. 1944. Amphibians and reptiles of the Chicago area. Chicago Nat. Hist. Mus. Press, Chicago.

Possardt, E. E. 1974. The breeding biology and larval development of the wood frog (*Rana sylvatica*). Dept. For. and Wildl. Manage., Univ. Mass., Amherst. Unpublished.

Pough, F. H. 1976. Acid precipitation and embryonic mortality of spotted salamanders (*Ambystoma maculatum*). *Science* 192:68–70.

Pough, F. H., and R. E. Wilson. 1976. Acid precipitation and reproductive success of *Ambystoma* salamanders. Pp. 531–44. In *Proceedings of the First International Symposium on Acid Precipitation and The Forest Ecosystem,* edited by L. S. Dochinger and T. A. Seliga, U.S. Dept. Agric. For. Serv. Gen. Tech. Rep. NE–23.

Powders, V. N., and W. L. Tietjen. 1974. The comparative food habits of sympatric and allopatric salamanders, *Plethodon glutinosus* and *Plethodon jordani* in eastern Tennessee and adjacent areas. *Herpetologica* 30:167–75.

R

Rand, A. S. 1950. Leopard frogs in caves in winter. *Copeia* 1950(4):324.

Raney, E. C. 1940. Summer movements of the bullfrog, *Rana catesbeiana* (Shaw), as determined by the jaw-tag method. *Am. Midl. Nat.* 23:733–45.

Raney, E. C., and R. M. Roecker. 1947. Food and growth of two species of watersnakes from western New York. *Copeia* 1947(3):171–74.

Richmond, N. D. 1947. Life history of *Scaphiopus h. holbrookii* (Harlan). Pt. 1: Larval development and behavior. *Ecology* 28:53–67.

Ries, K. M., and E. D. Bellis. 1966.

Spring food habits of the red-spotted newt in Pennsylvania. *Herpetologica* 22:152–55.

Risely, P. L. 1932. Observations on the natural history of the common musk turtle, *Sternotherus odoratus* (Latreille). *Pap. Mich. Acad. Sci., Arts and Letters* 17:685–711.

Rossman, D. A. 1970. *Thamnophis sauritus* (Linnaeus). *Cat. Am. Amphib. Rept.* 99.1–99.2.

S

Schaaf, R. T., Jr., and P. W. Smith. 1971. *Rana palustris* (LeConte). *Cat. Am. Amphib. Rept.* 117.1–117.3.

Schlauch, F. C. 1975. Agonistic behavior in a suburban Long Island population of the smooth green snake, *Opheodrys vernalis. Engelhardtia* 6(2):25–26.

Schmidt, K. P., and D. D. Davis. 1941. *Field book of snakes.* New York: G. P. Putnam and Sons.

Seibert, H. C., and C. W. Hagen, Jr. 1947. Studies on a population of snakes in Illinois. *Copeia* 1947(1):6–22.

Semlitsch, R. D. 1980a. Geographic and local variation in population parameters of the slimy salamander (*Plethodon glutinosus*). *Herpetologica* 36:6–16.

———. 1980b. Terrestrial activity and summer home range of the mole salamander (*Ambystoma talpoideum*). *Can. J. Zool.* 59:315–22.

Sexton, O. J. 1959. Spatial and temporal movements of a population of the painted turtle, *Chrysemys picta marginata* (Agassiz). *Ecol. Monogr.* 29:113–40.

Shoop, C. R. 1965. Orientation of *Ambystoma maculatum:* movements to and from breeding ponds. *Science* 149:558–59.

———. 1968. Migratory orientation of *Ambystoma maculatum:* movements near breeding ponds and displacements of migrating individuals. *Biol. Bull.* 135:230–38.

———. 1974. Yearly variation in larval survival of *Ambystoma maculatum. Ecology* 55:440–44.

Shoop, C. R., and G. E. Gunning. 1967. Seasonal activity and movements of *Necturus* in Louisiana. *Copeia* 1967(4):732–37.

Smith, H. M. 1946. *Handbook of lizards.* Ithaca, N.Y.: Comstock.

———. 1956. *Handbook of amphibians and reptiles of Kansas.* 2d ed. Mus. Nat. Hist.,

Misc. Publ. No. 9 Univ. Kansas Publ., Topeka.

———. 1978. *Amphibians of North America: a guide to field identification.* Racine, Wisc.: Western Publ. Co., Inc.

Smith, P. W. 1961. The amphibians and reptiles of Illinois. *Illinois Nat. Hist. Surv. Bull.* 28:1–298.

———. 1963. *Plethodon cinereus. Cat. Am. Amphib. Rept.* 5.1–5.3.

Stein, R. J. 1980. Species account form for: Second symposium on endangered and threatened plants and animals of New Jersey. Unpublished.

Stewart, D. 1974. *Canadian endangered species.* Toronto: Gage Publ.

Stewart, M. M. 1956a. Certain aspects of the natural history and development of the northern two-lined salamander, *Eurycea b. bislineata* (Green), in the Ithaca, New York region. Ph.D. diss., Cornell Univ. [From Diss. Abstr. 16(12):2567, 1956.]

———. 1956b. The separate effects of food and temperature differences on development of marbled salamander larvae. *J. Elisha Mitchell Sci. Soc.* 72:47–56.

———. 1961. Biology of the Allegany Indian Reservation and vicinity. Pt. 3: the amphibians, reptiles and mammals. *New York State Mus. Sci. Serv. Bull.* 383:63–88.

———. 1975. Habitat management in the Adirondack Park. *New York Environ. News* 2(17):1–2.

Stewart, M. M., and J. Rossi. 1981. The Albany Pine Bush: a northern outpost for southern species of amphibians and reptiles in New York. *Am. Midl. Nat.* 106:282–92.

Stewart, M. M., and P. Sandison. 1972. Comparative food habits of sympatric mink frogs, bullfrogs, and green frogs. *J. Herpetol.* 6:241–44.

Stickel, L. F. 1950. Population and home range relationships of the box turtle, *Terrapene c. carolina* (Linnaeus). *Ecol. Monogr.* 20:351–78.

Stickel, L. F., W. H. Stickel, and F. C. Schmid. 1980. Ecology of a Maryland population of black rat snakes *(Elaphe o. obsoleta). Am. Midl. Nat.* 103:1–14.

Stickel, W. H., and J. B. Cope. 1947. The home ranges and wanderings of snakes. *Copeia* 1947(2):127–36.

Stille, W. T. 1952. The nocturnal amphibian fauna of the southern Lake Michigan beach. *Ecology* 33:149–62.

———. 1954. Eggs of the salamander *Ambystoma jeffersonianum* in the Chicago area. *Copeia* 1954(4):300.

Stone, W. B., E. Kiviat, and S. A. Butkas. 1980. Toxicants in snapping turtles. *New York Fish and Game J.* 27:39–50.

Storer, D. H. 1840. A report on the reptiles of Massachusetts. *Boston Journ. Nat. Hist.* 3:1–64.

Strang, C. A. 1983. Spatial and temporal activity patterns in two territorial turtles. *J. Herpetol.* 17:43–47.

Surface, H. A. 1906. The serpents of Pennsylvania. *Penn. Dep. Agric. Div. Zool. Bull.* 4(4–5):113–202.

———. 1908. First report on the economic features of the turtles of Pennsylvania. *Penn. Dep. Agric. Div. Zool. Bull.* 6:105–196.

———. 1913. The amphibians of Pennsylvania. *Bimonthly Penn. Dep. Agric. Div. Zool. Bull.* 3(3–4):65–152, 1–11.

T

Taub, F. B. 1961. The distribution of the red-backed salamander, *Plethodon c. cinereus*, within the soil. *Ecology* 42:681–98.

Thompson, E. L., J. E. Gates, and G. J. Taylor. 1980. Distribution and breeding habitat selection of the Jefferson salamander, *Ambystoma jeffersonianum*, in Maryland. *J. Herpetol.* 14:113–20.

Thompson, Z. 1853. *Natural history of Vermont.* Reprint ed. Rutland, Vt.: Charles E. Tuttle Co., 1972.

Tilley, S. G. 1968. Size-fecundity relationships and their evolutionary implications in five desmognathine salamanders. *Evolution* 22:806–16.

———. 1970. Aspects of the reproductive and population ecology of *Desmognathus ochrophaeus* in the southern Appalachian mountains. Ph.D. diss., Univ. Mich. [From Diss. Abstr. Int. 31(8B):5084, 1971.]

———. 1972. Aspects of parental care and embryonic development in *Desmognathus ochrophaeus. Copeia* 1972(3):532–40.

———. 1973. *Desmognathus ochrophaeus. Cat. Am. Amphib. Rept.* 129.1–129.4.

Tilley, S. G., B. L. Lundrigan, and L. P. Brower. 1982. Erythrism and mimicry in the salamander *Plethodon cinereus. Herpetologica* 38:409–17.

Tinkle, D. W. 1961. Geographic variation in reproduction, size, sex ratio, and maturity of *Sternotherus odoratus* (Testudinata: Chelydridae). *Ecology* 42:68–76.

Trapido, H., and R. T. Clausen. 1938. Amphibians and reptiles of eastern Quebec. *Copeia* 1938(3):117–25.

U

Uhler, F. M., C. Cottom, and T. E. Clarke. 1939. Food of snakes of the George Washington National Forest, Virginia, in *Trans. Fourth North Am. Nat. Resour. and Wildl. Conf.*, pp. 605–22.

U.S. Department of Agriculture, Forest Service. 1977. *Forest statistics for the United States.* Washington, D.C.: Government Printing Office.

———, Soil Conservation Service. 1981. *Land resource regions and major land resource areas of the United States.* Agric. Handb., U.S. Dept. Agric., Soil Conserv. Serv.

U.S. Department of the Interior, Fish and Wildlife Service. 1980. *Endangered and threatened wildlife and plants—republication of list of species.* Federal Register 45(99):33768–33781.

Uzzell, T. M., Jr. 1964. Relations of the diploid and triploid species of the *Ambystoma jeffersonianum* complex (Amphibia, Caudata). *Copeia* 1964(2):257–300.

———. 1967a. *Ambystoma jeffersonianum. Cat. Am. Amphib. Rept.* 47.1–47.2.

———. 1967b. *Ambystoma laterale. Cat. Am. Amphib. Rept.* 48.1–48.2.

———. 1967c. *Ambystoma platineum. Cat. Am. Amphib. Rept.* 49.1–49.2.

———. 1967d. *Ambystoma tremblayi. Cat. Am. Amphib. Rept.* 50.1–50.2.

V

Verrill, A. E. 1863. Catalogue of the reptiles and batrachians found in the vicinity of Norway, Oxford County, Maine. *Proc. Boston Soc. Nat. Hist.* 9:195–99.

Vinegar, A., and M. Friedman. 1967. *Necturus* in Rhode Island. *Herpetologica* 23:51.

Vogt, R. C. 1981. *Natural history of amphibians and reptiles of Wisconsin.* Milwaukee: Milwaukee Public Museum.

W

Wacasey, J. W. 1961. An ecological study of two sympatric species of salamanders, *Ambystoma maculatum* and *Ambystoma jeffersonianum*, in southern Michigan.

Ph.D. diss., Mich. State Univ., East Lansing. [From Diss. Abstr. 23(1):368, 1962.]

Warfel, H. E. 1936. Notes on the occurrence of *Necturus maculosus* (Rafinesque) in Massachusetts. *Copeia* 1936(4):237.

Wasserman, A. O. 1968. *Scaphiopus holbrookii* (Harlan). *Cat. Am. Amphib. Rept.* 70.1–70.4.

Webb, R. G. 1961. Observations on the life histories of turtles (genus *Pseudemys* and *Graptemys*) in Lake Texoma, Oklahoma. *Am. Midl. Nat.* 56:193–214.

———. 1973. *Trionyx spiniferus* (LeSueur). *Cat. Am. Amphib. Rept.* 140.1–140.4.

Wells, K. D. 1976. Multiple egg clutches in the green frog *(Rana clamitans). Herpetologica* 32:85–87.

———. 1977. Territoriality and male mating success in the green frog *(Rana clamitans). Ecology* 58:750–62.

Wells, K. D., and R. A. Wells. 1976. Patterns of movement in a population of the slimy salamander, *Plethodon glutinosus,* with observations on aggregations. *Herpetologica* 32:156–62.

Whitford, A. G., and A. Vinegar. 1966. Homing, survivorship, and overwintering of larvae in *Ambystoma maculatum. Copeia* 1966(3):515–19.

Wilder, I. W. 1913. The life history of *Desmognathus fusca. Biol. Bull.* 24:251–342.

———. 1917. On the breeding habits of *Desmognathus fusca. Biol.* 32:13–20.

———. 1924. The relation of growth to metamorphosis in *Eurycea bislineata* (Green). *Journ. Exp. Zool.* 40:1–112.

Williams, J. E. 1952. Homing behavior of the painted turtle and musk turtle in a lake. *Copeia* 1952(2):76–82.

Williams, K. L. 1978. *Systematics and natural history of the American milk snake,* Lampropeltis triangulum. Milwaukee, Wisc.: Milwaukee Publ. Mus. Press.

Williams, P. K. 1973. Seasonal movements and population dynamics of four sympatric mole salamanders, genus *Ambystoma.* Ph.D. diss., Indiana Univ., Bloomington. (Information obtained from Semlitsch 1980b.)

Williams, T. K., and J. L. Christiansen. 1982. The niches of two sympatric softshell turtles, *Trionyx muticus* and *Trionyx spiniferus,* in Iowa. *J. Herpetol.* 15:303–8.

Wilson, L. D. 1978. *Coluber constrictor* (Linnaeus). *Cat. Am. Amphib. Rept.* 218.1–218.4.

Wilson, R. E. 1976. An ecological study of *Ambystoma maculatum* and *Ambystoma jeffersonianum.* Ph.D. diss., Cornell Univ., Ithaca, N.Y. (Information obtained from Thompson et al. 1980.)

Wood, J. T. 1953. Observations on the complements of ova and nesting of the four-toed salamander in Virginia. *Am. Nat.* 87:77–86.

Wood, W., 1634. *New-England's Prospect.* London. Reprint ed. Boston: Publ. of the Prince Society, 1865.

Woodward, B. D. 1982. Local intraspecific variation in clutch parameters in the spotted salamander *(Ambystoma maculatum). Copeia* 1982(1):157–60.

Wright, A. H. 1914. *North American Anura: life histories of the Anura of Ithaca, New York.* Carnegie Inst., Washington, D.C., Publ. No. 197.

Wright, A. H., and A. A. Allen. 1909. The early breeding habits of *Ambystoma punctatum. Am. Midl. Nat.* 43:687–92.

Wright, A. H., and A. A. Wright. 1949. *Handbook of frogs and toads.* Ithaca, N.Y.: Comstock.

———. 1957. *Handbook of snakes.* 2 vol. Ithaca, N.Y.: Comstock.

Z

Zappalorti, R. T. 1975. Herpetological associated data on field and laboratory observation. Unpublished.

Zappalorti, R. T., and R. F. Farrell. 1980. An ecological study of the bog turtle, *Clemmys muhlenbergii,* Schoepff (Reptilia, Testudines, Emydidae), in New Jersey, Pt. 3. Report to the New Jersey Dept. of Environ. Protection, Endangered and Nongame Spec. Proj., Federal Aid Prog. and Herpetological Associates. HA Rept. No. 80.01. Unpublished.

Zappalorti, R. T., R. F. Farrell, and E. M. Zanelli. 1979. The ecology and distribution of the bog turtle, *Clemmys muhlenbergii* Schoepff, in New Jersey, Pt. 2. Report to the New Jersey Dept. of Environ. Protection, Endangered and Nongame Spec. Proj., Federal Aid Prog. and Herpetological Associates. HA Rept. No. 79.02, Vol. 1, 38 pp. Unpublished.

Zehr, D. R. 1962. Stages in the normal development of the common garter snake, *Thamnophis sirtalis sirtalis. Copeia* 1962(2):322–29.

Zenisek, C. J. 1964. A study of the natural history and ecology of the leopard frog, *Rana pipiens* Schreber. Ph.D. diss., Ohio State Univ. [From Diss. Abstr. Int. 24(7):3035, 1964.]

Glossary

Aestivation. Reduction of biological activity by an organism, usually as a response to high temperatures or scarcity of water.

Arboreal. Tree inhabiting or adapted to living in trees.

Autotomy. Reflex separation of a part from the body; a division of the body into two or more pieces.

Carapace. The bony or chitinous dorsal shield covering a turtle's back.

Carnivorous. Feeding chiefly on animal tissues.

Cloaca. The common chamber into which the intestinal, urinary, and generative canals discharge.

Community. An association of interacting populations, usually delimited by their interactions or spatial (i.e., physiographic) occurrence.

Crepuscular. Active at twilight.

Ecotone. A habitat created by the juxtaposition of distinctly different habitats; an edge habitat.

Endangered. Describing a species whose habitat is threatened with destruction, drastic modification, or severe curtailment, or whose population is threatened because of overexploitation, disease, or other factors, and whose survival therefore requires assistance.

Fossorial. Adapted to digging; burrowing.

Gene pool. The sum of the genetic information carried by all individuals of a population.

Glacial moraine. An accumulation of earth and stones carried and finally deposited by a glacier.

Habitat. The place where an animal or plant normally lives, often characterized by a dominant plant form or physical characteristic (e.g., forest habitat, marsh habitat). Special habitat requirements are the key components needed by a given species in order to thrive.

Herbivorous. Feeding chiefly on plants.

Herpetofauna. The amphibians and/or reptiles inhabiting a given area.

Hibernation. Reduction of biological activity by organisms during winter; a state of torpidity as a response to low temperature.

Home range. An area from which intruders (usually conspecifics) may or may not be excluded and to which an animal restricts most of its normal activities (see *Territory*).

Insectivorous. Feeding chiefly on insects.

Intergrade. Populations intermediate in character between adjacent populations. The adjacent populations remain distinct.

Krummholz. The transition zone from subalpine forest to alpine tundra, as on a mountain slope, characterized by dwarfed, deformed, wind-sheared trees.

Larva. The early form of an animal that at birth or hatching is fundamentally unlike the adult form and must metamorphose before assuming adult characteristics.

Metamorphosis. An abrupt change in form during development that alters the function of an organism; transformation.

Neotenic. Retaining a larval or embryonic characteristic in the adult form; attaining sexual maturity during the larval stage.

Oviparous. Producing eggs that develop and hatch outside the body.

Oviposition. The deposition of eggs.

pH. A scale of acidity/alkalinity ranging from 1 to 14: values below 7 indicate acidity, values above, alkalinity.

Philipatry. Tendency of sexually mature animals to return to the locale of their birth or hatching.

Piscivorous. Feeding chiefly on fish.

Plastron. The ventral part of the shell of a tortoise or turtle, usually consisting of symmetrically arranged bones overlaid by horny plates.

Relative abundance: abundant (very plentiful); *common* (readily found to be present); *uncommon* (not readily found, but present); *rare* (present in such low numbers that a finding is considered noteworthy).

Riparian. Used to describe the banks and areas—including their vegetation—adjacent to natural water courses, seeps, and springs. (These water sources provide soil moisture sufficiently in excess of that otherwise available locally, so as to furnish a moister and, therefore, different habitat than that of contiguous flood plains and uplands.)

Scavenger. Feeding chiefly on carrion.

Scute. External epidermal bony or horny plate or scale, as on a turtle's shell.

Sexually mature. Fully developed biologically; able to reproduce; adult.

Species. A category of taxonomic classification comprising members of a potentially interbreeding population reproductively isolated from other such groups; an independent evolutionary unit.

Subspecies. Subpopulations within a species that are distinguishable by morphological or physiological characteristics.

Sympatric. Occurring in the same place, usually referring to overlap in species distributions.

Territory. Any area defended by one or more individuals against intrusion by others of the same or different species (see *Home range*).

Viviparous. Producing living young from within the body.

Index